Demons, Deliverance, and Discernment

Separating Fact from Fiction About the Spirit World

FR. MIKE DRISCOLL

Demons, Deliverance, and Discernment

Separating Fact from Fiction About the Spirit World

Published by Catholic Answers, Inc.
2020 Gillespie Way
El Cajon, California 92020
1-888-291-8000 orders
619-387-0042 fax
catholic.com

Printed in the United States of America

Cover design by Devin Schadt
Interior design by Sherry Russell

978-1-941663-20-2
978-1-941663-21-9 Kindle
978-1-941663-22-6 ePub

Be sober, be watchful. Your adversary the devil prowls around like a roaring lion, seeking someone to devour. Resist him, firm in your faith.

1 Peter 5:8–9

Contents

Why Do We Need Another Book on Demonic Possession?

Catholic books on the topic of demonic possession fall into three categories. The first is demonology, or the study of demons. Books in this category talk about the nature and activity of demons, one small part of which is the study of possession and exorcism.

Then there have been a few books written by exorcists. These also cover demonology, but focus more on possession and exorcism. They have the advantage of being first-hand accounts, written by priests who were authorized by bishops to perform exorcisms. They place heavy emphasis on topics that are bound to attract attention, including astonishing stories of preternatural occurrences accompanying demon possession, types of and particular demons they have confronted, and their methods of exorcism

A third group of books on demonic possession comprises those written by Catholics claiming expertise on identifying and fighting demonic attacks that fall short of possession. These authors have no official standing in the Church, and their explanations and methods are not taken from any Catholic authority. Like the books written by exorcists, these emphasize first-hand stories and descriptions of the means that must be employed to deliver people from demonic attacks.

I wanted to write a different kind of book.

As a priest with a doctorate in counseling, I wish to give attention to an area that is often left out of other Catholic books about exorcism, and certainly out of mainstream cultural treatment of demonology: identifying and recognizing the differences between demonic activity and mental disorders. Not all personal problems, even serious ones, have a demon behind them, and the Church has never taught that they do.

Furthermore, I am not an exorcist, so I don't have exciting first-hand stories of demonic attacks. In the course of my research, however, I heard many such stories from experienced exorcists (who wish to remain anonymous). These stories can be necessary reminders to us that Satan and his demons really do operate in our world, sometimes in extraordinary ways, and in this book I will share some of them where appropriate.

Finally, I think that many books—Catholic and non-Catholic—about possession and exorcism are written by authors who rely on claims of extraordinary spiritual gifts and self-made methods for identifying and fighting demonic assaults. I will critique this approach, and make the case for using only the Church's traditional methods.

Demons, Mental Disorders, and Discernment

One study of 488 different cultures found that three-quarters of them have institutionalized beliefs in spirit possession of human beings.[1] There are several possibilities that might explain reported phenomena of possession and exorcism. The first is that they are real: that sometimes individuals actually become possessed by spirits, and these spirits can be expelled through exorcism rituals. A second is that alleged occurrences of spirit possession are the result of mental disorders, role-playing, or the power of suggestion. According to this theory, exorcisms may be effective only as a placebo for those who believe themselves possessed or are mentally disturbed. A third possibility is that people are able to enter an altered state of consciousness that resembles possession and is concluded by exorcism rituals.[2] A final alternative is that any given alleged case of spirit possession is simply a hoax.

Although different alleged cases of possession may be explained by any of these, only the first possibility—that spirit possession is a real thing—can explain incidents that defy natural explanation. The other theories must leave such episodes as unsolved mysteries. This book is written from the point of view that possession by spirits—particularly evil spirits, also known as fallen angels or devils—is real.

About the time I finished a master of arts in counseling, I had a few conversations with an exorcist I had known for years. I had become familiar with the diagnosis of mental disorders, and I had read a little on the topic of demonic possession—but only a little. I don't remember it coming up in my seminary courses. It probably was mentioned, but scant time was spent on it, and rightfully so. Most priests are never going to perform an exorcism. I would also say that most priests are never going to see a possessed person, but the different opinions on that point are part of the study of this book.

As soon as I finished that degree, I was accepted into a Ph.D. program called *Counselor Education and Supervision*. As before, I had courses on emotional and mental disorders, relationship difficulties, life problems, and how to help people deal with them. However, we also spent time studying counselors: how to teach them, supervise them, and help them deal with their own struggles. Early in the program, I thought it would be interesting to take a similar approach toward research on possession and exorcism. I decided to study not just those topics, but also the exorcists themselves. How did they get involved in performing exorcisms—something that less than one priest in a thousand ever does? What training did they undergo? And last but not least, what makes them conclude that a particular person is suffering from demon possession rather than from a mental disorder? I decided to do my doctoral dissertation on this subject. After defending the dissertation and finishing the degree, I proceeded to write this book.

In summary, I wrote it to address three questions: How do Catholic exorcists discern possession? How do they perform exorcisms? How do Catholics address lower level demonic attacks? Depending upon who is asked, there are different answers to these questions. The answers affect all of us in our daily struggles against the enemy. Although we may not face the more dramatic demonic attacks, the devil tempts *everyone*—he even tempted our Lord. We would be mistaken if we acted as if demonic possession were commonplace. We would be equally mistaken, however—as well as foolish—to ignore the presence of the devil, and to neglect the means of resisting his activity in the world. In the Rite of Baptism, those being baptized (or their godparents) promise to *renounce Satan, and all his works, and all his empty promises.* We should make it a daily spiritual practice to fulfill these promises. I hope this book will help you do so.

1

Spirit Possession Worldwide

When we hear the word *possession*, we often think of evil spirits forcibly taking control of a person's body in a harmful way. Numerous cultures have similar beliefs about possession by evil spirits, but many of these cultures also maintain that people can be possessed in a desirable and voluntary way by good spirits. In this chapter, we look at stories of possession and exorcism in non-Christian cultures throughout the world. As we will see, there are similarities between Catholic beliefs and certain aspects of pagan religions in regard to spirit possession and exorcism.

What Are the Possessing Spirits?

The Catholic Faith teaches that the only beings with immortal souls are God, angels, and human beings.[3] Good angels are found in heaven and on earth; fallen angels are found in hell and on earth. The souls of dead human beings are either in heaven, hell, or purgatory.[4] Historically, the majority of Christians have shared most of these beliefs regarding the spirit world.

Non-Christian cultures have a wide variety of beliefs regarding possessing spirits. They believe spirits may be good, evil, or—like human beings—a combination of good and evil. Other spirits, like those of animals, have no moral bearing one way or the other. The experience of being possessed generally corresponds with the moral nature of the spirit. Possession by good spirits is often pleasant and desirable; possession by evil spirits is unpleasant and undesirable; possession by amoral spirits or those of mixed moral character can go either way.

Some cultures believe that gods may be possessing spirits. These may be male or female, weak or powerful, good or evil. The spirits of ancestors or cultural heroes are also believed to possess individuals. The possessed person is believed to acquire either temporarily or permanently some of the spirit's characteristics. Possession by animal spirits is yet another belief. The victims of this type of possession are said to behave like an animal, and their faces may even contort to look like it. Finally, some cultures have beliefs in spirit possession without any clear indication of what the spirit is. In these cases, the definition of spirit possession is met as long as an immaterial, outside entity exerts strong influence or control over its victim.

Who Becomes Possessed?

Many cultures believe that spirits may possess willing individuals during ritual worship. These cases of possession are generally considered neutral or even positive experiences. Involuntary possession, on the other hand, may result from something the possessed person did to deserve it. For example, the spirits of those who died during feuds or disputes may possess their enemies until the situation is resolved. Likewise, if the relatives of a deceased person fail to perform proper ceremonies, the offended spirit may use possession as a means to force the family to provide the appropriate honors.

However, certain cultures believe that people might become spirit-possessed through no fault of their own. Spirits who died tragically or who are being punished for sins of their earthly life are believed to possess people randomly.

These spirits may be attached to a particular place and possess passersby, or they may wander aimlessly before attacking an innocent victim. Some societies also believe that particular human beings have the power to cause spirit possession by casting a spell or curse.

STORIES OF SPIRIT POSSESSION

There are innumerable stories of spirit possession in different cultures throughout the world. I have chosen the following examples to illustrate the variety of spirit possession beliefs that exist.

TRINIDAD: *KALI, THE GODDESS OF GOOD HEALTH*[5]

In the West Indies island of Trinidad, some inhabitants worship a number of gods and goddesses. There is one called *Kali,* who is the goddess that the islanders invoke to protect them against smallpox and other diseases. Every spring, the priests of this goddess have a ceremony in her honor. They prepare by abstaining from food and sexual relations the preceding night. Early the next morning they bathe themselves, carefully clean and sweep the outdoor area where the ceremony is held, and decorate it with flowers and pictures of the goddess. Members of the village prepare food both as an offering to Kali and for the communal feast that follows.

To begin the ritual, designated people chant, and one plays a drum. After about an hour, the priest, who until this moment had been sitting motionless, rises to his feet. He begins to speak in a harsh voice unlike his own, and expresses anger at the islanders over the preparations they had made. The goddess Kali, speaking through the priest, says the preparations are inadequate—as always. Individuals from the community then come forward, and meekly but directly ask for answers and advice; for example, why sickness and other evils had befallen them during the past year and what they should do about it. The angry voice of Kali tells them about the transgressions they have committed, which include everything from adultery to insufficient offerings in her honor. When the tribe members finish consulting the goddess, the ceremony concludes with an animal sacrifice. The possessing spirit then departs from the priest, who apparently does not remember what had happened. He is exhausted and is bedridden the rest of the day.

Tulu: *Siri, the Goddess of Prosperity*[6]

The Tulu culture of southern India has an annual ritual in which thousands of people honor Siri, the pagan goddess of prosperity. The eight-hour ritual includes bringing offerings to this goddess and chanting an ancient legend about her. During the ceremony women claim to be possessed by the spirit of Siri, while men are said to be possessed by the spirit of her son Kumar. Most participants seem to have a positive experience: they sway to the sound of the singing, become glassy eyed, and are said to establish a spiritual bond with one another. However, one or more of them—usually novices—scream incoherently, hiss, curse, throw themselves to the ground and become violent. Family members often claim that the victims of this more violent behavior have been acting this way for some length of time, as a result of possession by an evil spirit. An elder will instruct the victims and their families on how to avoid this possession, particularly by encouraging devotion to Siri. He concludes by chanting prayers and sprinkling holy water.

Sanpoil: *Guardian Spirits*[7]

The Sanpoil are a Native American tribe that inhabited the area that is now the upper northwest United States. They currently live on a reservation in Washington State. The Sanpoil have traditionally believed in guardian spirits that help them through life. Adolescents were sent away from home to be alone for a time, during which their guardian spirit would reveal itself. During their mid-winter ceremony in honor of the guardian spirits, novices would become possessed by their spirits. However, possibly for malicious reasons, the leader or elder might disrupt the process by sending one of his own guardian spirits to possess a novice. This could cause delirium or insanity, and result in the novice speaking in the voice of the elder.

Shona: *Ancestor Spirits*[8]

The Shona religion of Zimbabwe has a well-defined belief in ancestral spirits. When a person dies and is buried, a long stick is inserted into the ground above the grave. After some months of allowing the earth to settle, the family removes the stick, leaving a deep, narrow hole. Family members then visit the grave frequently, waiting to see a caterpillar crawl out of the hole. When they see this, it means that the spirit of the deceased has left the grave and is wandering, trying to return to its family. The family allows the spirit to wander for about a year, and then prepares a ritual to welcome it home.

On the chosen day, the family slaughters an animal as a sacrifice to the spirit, prepares a corn dish, and brews beer. The family members take these items to the grave, pour the beer upon the burial site, and leave the food. Participants then tell the spirit that it is welcome to rejoin the family.

They return home for a celebration, at which the spirit of the deceased possesses one of the family members. The final stage of the ceremony takes place the next morning. The family takes a pot of beer to a cattle enclosure and pours it on a bull's head. They repeat this as often as necessary until the bull shakes its head, which is a sign that the spirit is now happy. The women then burst into ululation, a high-pitched trilling sound, celebrating their new ancestral spirit.

JAPAN: *FOX SPIRIT*

An example of possession by an animal spirit is the fascinating Japanese belief called *kitsune-tsuki*, which means being possessed by the spirit of a *kitsune* or fox. There are ancient stories in Japan about the fox being an intelligent and powerful creature, whose spirit sometimes takes possession of young women.[9] The fox spirit enters from beneath a woman's fingernails or through her breasts. She might fall to the ground, and foam at the mouth, and a swelling or lump may appear beneath her skin and move around her body. Her face may contort to resemble a fox; she may utter a foxlike bark; and she may have a strong appetite for the foods that foxes are believed to like, especially rice and tofu. She might also run wildly (and nakedly) through her village. If she is illiterate, she may instantly acquire the ability to read and write; if literate, she may suddenly possess knowledge of a language that she did not previously know. According to one belief, fox spirits are connected to *Inari*, the god of rice.[10] In order to free the victim of *kitsune-tsuki*, the family of the possessed might say special prayers to this god, asking him to relieve the victim. If that failed, the possessed individual could be taken to an Inari shrine, where the priest would recommend a cure. Sometimes more drastic steps were sometimes taken:

the community might drive the victim and her family out of the village, or even burn or kill them.[11]

HUNGARY: *TALTOS CHILDREN*[12]

In Hungary, adolescents who are thought to be spiritually sensitive in some way are called *taltos* children. It is a common experience among *taltos* children to become socially withdrawn, uncommunicative with family, and to run away from home. They normally return battered and bruised, their clothing in tatters, claiming they have experienced a spiritual possession or altered state of consciousness.

MURNGIN: *CHILD SPIRITS*[13]

The Murngin tribe of Arnhem Land (northern Australia) believes in a type of spirit possession that leads to childbirth. Prior to his conception, the spirit of a child appears to his father in a dream or as part of some other mystical experience. This spirit asks the father to identify his mother, then enters the woman through her vagina, causing her to become pregnant. Since the Murngin people are well aware of the biological cause of conception, it seems the tribe members view this belief as the spiritual cause of conceiving a child.

EXORCISM IN WORLD CULTURES

Positive spirit possession, which is voluntary and desirable, generally takes place as part of a pagan religious ritual. The spirit takes possession of one or more individuals as part of the ceremony, and departs at the conclusion of the ceremony. Negative spirit possession, on the other hand, is involuntary, undesirable, and unpleasant. These spirits often depart during a religious ritual, but they must be forced to leave the victim (or convinced through negotiation) rather than leaving of their volition. This ritual of expelling unwanted spirits from individuals is called *exorcism*.

The exorcist, the person conducting the exorcism ceremony, is believed to have a special authority, experience, or ability to interact with the spirit world. In some cultures only men may be exorcists, but there are also cultures in which most exorcists are women. Some exorcists prepare themselves for the exorcism ceremony through prayer, fasting, and other purifying rituals. The exorcist prepares a special place for the ceremony by praying, arranging decorations, and assembling the necessary accessories, including: fire, water, oil, incense; bells, drums, and other musical instruments; offerings of food, drink, plants, and animals. Some exorcists wear masks, which they believe enhance their ability to communicate with or battle the spirits. Prayers, incantations, and dancing are also typically part of the ritual.

During the ceremony, victims may exhibit wild behavior such as screaming, moaning, clawing themselves until bloody, and slamming their bodies or heads against a wall or other objects. In other cases they may become motionless and rigid, and appear to be unconscious. If the exorcist repeatedly performs the ceremony over a length of days or weeks, these behaviors may continue between the sessions. If the exorcism takes place indoors, the room may undergo disturbances such as unexplainable noises, shaking walls, and displaced objects. One anthropologist even reported a sudden invasion of spiders.[14]

By definition, possessing spirits do not have physical bodies. Nevertheless, when taking possession of or departing from a victim, they are sometimes believed to have a vague material quality. They have been said to enter or leave through the victim's mouth, ears, fingers, toes, or through a cut in the skin.

Appeasing Offended Spirits

A ritual in which the exorcist negotiates with or tries to appease the possessing spirit may be called an *appeasement* exorcism. It is performed when individuals are believed to be possessed by good (or neutral) spirits that have been disrespected. The possessing spirits may be those of dead people who are looking for revenge against enemies who harmed them during life, or seeking justice from relatives who did not perform the proper ceremonies at their death. They may also be inhuman spirits of places or things, such as trees, rivers, or ponds, retaliating against a disturbance by possessing the offender.

In these cases, the exorcist performs a ceremony to apologize for the offense and to make amends. The ceremony may be employed after the exorcist has communicated with the spirit, or the ceremony itself may be the means of communication. The exorcist may enter into a trance, and his voice may change to indicate that the offended spirit is speaking through him. The victim of the possessing spirit is almost always present for the ceremony, and often the victim's family, clan, village, or tribe is also present. The ceremony itself, with its prayers and offerings, may be enough to appease the spirits. Otherwise, the ceremony may reveal to the exorcist the offended spirit's additional demands.

Fiji Appeasement Exorcism[15]

An example of an appeasement type of exorcism gained local attention in the Fiji Islands in 1968. A local man named

Munsami had been one of the leaders in an effort to build a new school. In the construction process, he damaged a natural rock formation that held what was believed to be a sacred pool of water. Shortly after the school was completed, Munsami was afflicted by a severe skin disease, and died three years later. Immediately after his death, eighteen schoolgirls from ages eight through fourteen began having identical health problems. They experienced irregular breathing and hyperventilation, their arms and hands twitched, and they made high-pitched growling sounds. The villagers attributed both Munsami's death and the girls' illness to the spirits of the pool being offended by the damage done to the rock formation. Local Western physicians investigated and found that the girl most severely afflicted had a history of emotional problems and hyperventilating. The doctors came to the conclusion that when the young girl, whom the doctors referred to as the trigger girl, went through an episode, it triggered similar behavior in some of her classmates. The doctors were able to relieve the situation by closing the school for a week, and telling the girls' parents to keep them separated from one another.

The parents and villagers were not convinced that this was enough. They consulted a local Muslim healer, who agreed that the spirits were offended. She ordered that kava fruit be offered to the spirits at the pool, accompanied by traditional Fiji prayers. While this was being done, she had the girls brought to her and rubbed their throats with coconut oil. The rite helped temporarily, but the girls' afflictions resumed shortly after they left the healer.

The parents then contacted the Hindu healer at a temple near their village. Upon arriving at the school, he prayed to the Hindu god Ganesh to protect the school. He said that he felt no evil spirits, but perceived that the good spirits of the pool were angry at being disturbed. He asked that the girls be brought to the pool, and tied a talisman as a necklace on each of them. He burned camphor, poured milk into the pool, and poured a kava fruit concoction around it, asking the angry spirits to forgive the offense that had been done to their pool. At its conclusion, he told the villagers that the ceremony had satisfied the spirits; they were no longer angry, and would no longer afflict the girls.

However, the villagers decided to hold a prayer ceremony to be even more certain of a permanent cure for the girls. The villagers prepared a sacred place on the school playground by cutting the grass and spreading cow manure on it, then dug a fire pit and filled it with dried mango twigs. They also prepared food that would serve as an offering as well as a sacred feast. During the elaborate ritual, a Hindu priest prayed, the afflicted girls poured butter into the fire, and everyone present shared a sacred meal. They concluded the rite by collecting what was left in the fire pit and placing it under a sacred mango tree.

The one girl who did not take part in these rituals was the so-called trigger girl, the one whose problems had preceded the others. The Western physicians had been treating her all along, with mixed results. In contrast, within two days of the great village ceremony, all of the other girls were completely relieved of their symptoms.

BATTLING EVIL SPIRITS

That story is an example of an appeasement exorcism in which offended spirits seek justice. In these, after the exorcist offers ceremonies of apology and reparation, the spirits end their possession. A different type of exorcism is performed when the exorcist believes the possessing spirits are inherently evil and must be forced to depart. Those evil spirits may possess and torment people at random; they may inhabit a particular place, and attack those who happen by; they may possess their victims as the result of a curse or spell cast by an enemy of the victim; or they may possess individuals who—either deliberately or mistakenly—enter into relationships with them. Because the exorcist must fight the possessing spirits rather than appease them, these can be called *battle* exorcisms.

In battle exorcisms, the victims may have opened themselves to the possessing spirit or provoked it in some way, but the spirit has no interest in accepting any apology, offering, or other means of making amends. Therefore, the exorcist and the possessing spirit interact as enemies. The exorcist recites prayers or incantations, and carries out elaborate rituals that are believed to force the spirits out of the victim. The exorcist often demands from the evil spirits their names and number; how, why, and when they entered the victim; the means by which they might be driven out; and the sign that will occur to confirm the exorcism. The victims of spirit possession are almost always present for the exorcism ceremony, as are some family members. Others in the tribe or clan may also be present, although this is not as important as in the appeasement exorcism, since only the efforts of the exorcist can successfully drive it from the victim.

In some cultures the ritual may involve a mask, a figurine, a small statue, or another object.[16] In these ceremonies, the exorcist forces the spirit to leave its victim and enter the object, which then may be destroyed (often by fire) or sealed with prayers or incantations, thereby imprisoning the spirit within it. The exorcist gauges the success of the ceremony by observing whether or not the victims have been restored to the physical, mental, emotional, and spiritual state they were in before the possession occurred. When these ceremonies fail, there have been rare but tragic cases in which the exorcist and/or the community have beaten, burned, suffocated, or otherwise injured the victims, sometimes causing their death.[17]

HAITI BATTLE EXORCISM[18]

An example of a battle exorcism was witnessed by a French anthropologist in Haiti in 1959. A healthy man had suddenly become ill and was unable to eat, to such an extent that he was wasting away. Because his family believed that this was the result of his being possessed by an evil spirit, he was taken to a sacred house where the exorcist prepared a mat for him and placed it on some ashes and coffee grounds. The man took off his shirt and lay down on the mat. The exorcist said some prayers, threw bile from a bull on the man's face and body, spat rum into his face, and pounded his arms and legs. Later, he was taken outside; placed in a trench; and rubbed with herbal water, oil, and flaming rum. The ceremony concluded with the man getting out of the trench and a chicken being buried alive in it. Afterward, the exorcist gave the man a clean shirt to wear, a cup of tea to drink, and told him to spit a lot. Subsequently, the man quickly regained his health.

COMPARISON OF PAGAN AND CATHOLIC BELIEFS

When Christians hear of spirit possession, we often think immediately of demonic possession. Perhaps this is due to the fact that the Catholic Church, along with nearly all Christian denominations, recognizes only this type of spirit possession. Although Christians do not usually identify the activity of the Holy Spirit in a believer's life as possession, it does have parallels in the positive spirit possession experiences found in other cultures. Note that in the Fiji appeasement exorcism described above, the exorcist sensed that the spirits were good but angry; he communicated with them to learn why they were angry and what should be done to placate them. He did not need to do anything to the victims, other than tie a talisman around their necks. In the Haitian battle exorcism, the exorcist sensed that the spirit was evil, so there was no attempt to negotiate with or satisfy it. Instead, the ceremony appeared to drive it out by brute force, as seen by the bile thrown on the victim and the pounding given to his arms and legs.

Catholic beliefs regarding demon possession and exorcism have certain similarities with pagan battle exorcisms. Both the Catholic exorcism ritual and pagan exorcism hold that there should be no attempt to negotiate with or appease the spirits, since the spirits are wholly evil; the exorcist must forcibly drive out the spirits. Both Catholicism and paganism maintain that possession can be the result of a curse or spell, or by the neglect of religious obligations. Both may see as signs of possession phenomena such as a trance-like state, convulsions, shouting and cursing, speaking a previously unknown language, personality changes, physical or mental illness, and violence. Both Catholicism and paganism have exorcism ceremonies that may involve incense, holy water, prayers, and commands directed at the evil spirit. Perhaps most interesting is that both Catholic and pagan exorcists demand that the spirits reveal their names; how, why, and when they entered the victim; the means by which they may be driven out; and the sign that will show they have departed.

~

What, then, is the Catholic view of what is happening in these cross-cultural examples of pagan possession and exorcism? To answer this we must look at three things.

First, how do the particular pagan beliefs about possessing spirits compare with Catholic teaching? Catholics do not believe in possession by any spirits other than demons: whether animals, dead human beings, or gods. That said, demons can masquerade as any of the spirits found in pagan beliefs—even as an angel of light (2 Cor. 11:14).

A second thing to examine is whether there can be pagan experiences of spirit possession that are entirely positive. Since the only spiritual beings with whom we should interact are God, his angels, and the saints, we must be cautious of any practice that invokes other beings in the spirit world. Non-Christians may be sincere in their beliefs regarding positive spirit possession, but these beliefs are false, and potentially dangerous. One should view these pagan practices as a grab bag, with people reaching around blindly in the hope that they will latch on to something worthwhile. Sometimes they succeed, sometimes they don't, and sometimes their hands get bitten by serpents.

Finally, we must ask whether pagan exorcisms can actually succeed in driving demons out of people who are truly possessed. One Catholic exorcist provides a good answer to this question by way of a comparison with a dying man in the desert looking for water. The man may have no choice but to drink from the first pool of water he sees, and it may save him from dying of thirst, but that same water may also be contaminated with germs that cause sickness and death. Similarly, pagans facing demonic possession may have no real option other than to seek help from their own priest, shaman, or other kind of exorcist. If he is a good person acting sincerely to the best of his knowledge, God may reward his efforts by expelling the demons from the possessed person. If not, the interaction with the spirit world could invoke demons and make matters worse.

We have finished our look at examples of pagan belief in regard to spirit possession and exorcism. The next chapter turns to universal Christian beliefs regarding demonic possession, based on biblical teaching.

Demonic Attacks in the Bible

The creature known as the devil, Satan, or Lucifer is the leader of all evil spirits (Isa. 14:12–15; Rev. 12:9). These evil spirits are angels, intelligent and powerful beings that God created inherently good. Some of them made a free and permanent decision to reject God, and were driven from heaven by God and by the spirits loyal to him. As a result of their rebellion, the evil spirits—otherwise known as demons, or sometimes, devils—became the enemies of the human race (Luke 10:18; John 12:31–32; Rev. 12:7–17).

DEMONS IN THE OLD TESTAMENT

In reading through the Bible, it is striking how much more frequently demonic attacks and exorcisms appear in the New Testament than in the Old Testament. St. Thomas Aquinas thought it was because the Israelites kept abandoning the worship of God and turning toward false idols.[19] If the Old Testament books had referenced evil spirits, he thought, the Israelites would have been tempted to worship them. As we consider our Western society, in which people pursue all kinds of false idols and false spiritual practices, it is difficult to disagree with Aquinas.

The first appearance of the devil in the Old Testament, and probably the best known, is from the book of Genesis: "Now the serpent was more subtle than any other wild creature that the LORD God had made" (3:1). He proceeded to tempt Adam and Eve to sin, thereby causing humanity to lose the earthly paradise that God had given them. Some would say that the serpent is merely a symbol or illustration of the devil, thus maintaining that the devil was an invisible spirit when he spoke to Eve. However, Satan is certainly capable of taking control of an animal and communicating through it.

The Old Testament indicates that King Saul, possessed by an evil spirit that provoked him to rage and violence, repeatedly tried to kill David (1 Sam. 18:10 ff.). This reference is the first time that demonic possession is mentioned in the Bible. After David became king, the devil successfully enticed him to conduct a census in violation of God's prohibition (1 Chron. 21:1)—a case of temptation rather than possession.

Job's children were killed, his possessions destroyed and stolen, and his health severely weakened, all by the work of Satan (Job 1:6 ff.). As we will see later, the word *oppression* is sometimes used to explain demonic attacks of this kind, which are neither temptation nor possession.

Another example of this kind of violent demonic attack is found in the book of Tobit, in which the demon Asmodeus killed several husbands of Sarah before her marriage to Tobias (Tob. 6:7–17; 8:1–3). Also, in the book of the prophet Zechariah, Satan is mentioned as accusing the high priest Joshua in some undefined manner (Zech. 3:1–2). Furthermore, in some English translations of Scripture (for example, the Douay-Reims), Psalm 91:6 refers to the *noon-day devil*, which the Rite of Exorcism also mentions. Aside from a few additional passages of an ambiguous nature, this is the extent of any references to demonic attacks in the Old Testament.

THE DEVIL IN THE NEW TESTAMENT

The New Testament tells us that a central part of Jesus' work was to free the world from the dominion of Satan (Acts

10:38). Jesus said that Satan is a murderer from the beginning, a liar and the father of lies, and the ruler of this world (John 8:44; 12:31). After he entered Jerusalem on Palm Sunday, Jesus said that he would defeat the devil by his Crucifixion: "Now is the judgment of this world, now shall the ruler of this world be cast out" (John 12:31). When St. Paul was traveling to Damascus, Jesus appeared and sent him to the Gentiles, "to open their eyes, that they may turn from darkness to light and from the power of Satan to God" (Acts 26:18). Paul later wrote that, although the world was still subject to the power of Satan, this would end in God's time (Rom. 8:19–22). In his first epistle, St. John confirms, "The reason the Son of God appeared was to destroy the works of the devil" (1 John 3:8).

The Book of Revelation begins with Jesus addressing messages to the Church in seven different cities. In speaking to the Church in Smyrna, Jesus said that the devil would have some of them cast into prison (Rev. 2:10). In describing the evil of the city of Pergamum, Jesus called it the place "where Satan's throne is . . . [and] where Satan dwells" (Rev. 2:12–13). In writing to the church in Thyatira, Jesus calls false teachings "the deep things of Satan" (Rev. 2:24). Later in Revelation, Satan is symbolized as a dragon that attacks the Mother of God (Rev. 12:1–6). According to the biblical account, shortly after Satan and his followers rebelled against God, Michael and his angels defeated them in a great heavenly battle (Rev. 12:7–9). The fallen angels, thus cast out of heaven, continue their rebellion on earth by afflicting mankind (Rev. 12:17–13:9). In the battle at the end of the world, the Antichrist will use the power of the devil to launch the final rebellion against Christ and his Church. Only then will the devil be confined to hell for eternity (Rev. 19:19–20:10).

TEMPTATION

One type of demonic activity, sometimes called *ordinary* demonic activity because it is common, is *temptation*. Prior to the beginning of Jesus' public ministry, Satan tempted Jesus to misuse his divine power in various ways, even in the worship of Satan himself (Matt. 4:1–11). In this incident, we see an indication of the preternatural powers of the devil: Satan has the ability to transport Jesus from the desert into Jerusalem and to a mountaintop.

Elsewhere, Jesus and Paul gave general warnings regarding temptation to sin that come from Satan (Mark 4:15; 1 Cor. 7:5; 2 Cor. 2:11; 12:7; Eph. 6:11). St. Peter's description of demonic temptation is both colorful and frightening: "Be sober, be watchful. Your adversary the devil prowls around like a roaring lion, seeking someone to devour. Resist him, firm in your faith" (1 Pet. 5:8–9).

Specific cases of Satan tempting people to sin are also mentioned, including the occasion when Jesus rebuked Peter for suggesting that he avoid the cross: "Turning and seeing his disciples, he rebuked Peter, and said, 'Get behind me, Satan! For you are not on the side of God, but of men'" (Mark 8:33).

POSSESSION

More dramatic than temptations are the cases of possession described in the New Testament. One of the most notable is that which occurs in the Gerasene territory, in which hundreds of demons possessed two men (Matt. 8:28–32; Mark 5:1–15; Luke 8:26–33). These men lived among tombs; they shrieked, gashed themselves with stones, and broke handcuffs and chains. Another case is carefully described in which a child had convulsions, foamed at the mouth, ground his teeth, became rigid, and was thrown to the ground and into either fire or water, depending upon the account (Matt. 17:14–18; Mark 9:14–27; Luke 9:37–42). The New Testament describes this demon as being mute and deaf. Although it is not stated that the child was also mute and deaf, this seems to be the implication. In the New Testament, maladies attributed to possession include muteness (Matt. 9:32–33; Luke 11:14), blindness (Matt. 12:22), infirmity characterized by weakness, and the inability to stand straight (Luke 13:10–16).

Distinct from the other cases of possession in the New Testament is the possession of the apostle Judas. The Gospels of Luke and John indicate that the devil possessed Judas, entered him (or entered his heart), and thereby incited him to betray Jesus (Luke 22:3; John 13:27). For Judas the Bible records no visible signs of possession.

It is fascinating that virtually all of the cases of demon possession in the Gospels occur in the northern part of Israel, which covers Galilee and the surrounding area. In the southern parts of Israel, mainly Jerusalem and its immediate area of Judea, there are none. Reinforcing this difference is the contrasting geographical sites used by the Gospel writers. Matthew, Mark, and Luke wrote mainly about Jesus' activity in the north, and they record numerous instances of possession and exorcism, while John wrote chiefly about the south, and does not describe any.

Those who do not believe in the truth and accuracy of the Gospels offer an explanation of this: Jesus was not performing exorcisms, but was instead performing physical, mental, and/or emotional healings. The Sadducees, who did not believe in angels, influenced the Israelites in the southern portion of Judea. Therefore, these Israelites would not have believed in demons, possession, or exorcism, whereas the Jewish people in Galilee and northern Israel, who were not influenced by the Sadducees in the same way, attributed problems to demons. The Gospel writers simply reflected the beliefs of the place they were writing about, they say, so demon possession and exorcism are said to take place in Galilee and the north—but not in Jerusalem and the south.

This explanation doesn't work for those of us who believe the Holy Spirit divinely inspired the Gospel writers, thus guaranteeing the inerrancy of their accounts. There are other ways to explain why demon possession is described in Galilee rather than Judea. Maybe the Israelites in the north were influenced more directly by their pagan neighbors and thereby opened themselves to more demonic attacks. Maybe God gave special protection to the holy city of Jerusalem and the surrounding area.

Of course, the variance in Gospel accounts of demon activity does not require any explanation beyond the truism that there are four different Gospels. The many differences between the Gospels make them complementary, not contradictory. For example, in the Last Supper narratives, John is the only evangelist who does not recount the institution of the Eucharist, and is also the only one to describe Jesus washing the feet of his apostles. Each of the evangelists included and excluded material in the life of Christ as the Holy Spirit inspired him. The point to remember in regard to demonic possession and exorcism is that the lack of such accounts in John's Gospel is no reason to doubt what the other evangelists wrote about such incidents.

EXORCISM

The New Testament depicts Jesus frequently performing exorcisms (Matt. 8:16; Mark 1:32–34; Luke 6:18). He did so simply by a word of command (Matt. 8:16), with the notable exception being the time that he laid hands upon a woman

(Luke 13:10–13). The most unusual exorcism Christ performed was in the incident of the Gerasene demoniac, in which the demons begged Jesus to allow them to enter a herd of pigs. When he did so, the demons possessed the animals and caused them to run off a bluff and drown themselves in the sea (Matt. 8:28–32; Mark 5:1–15; Luke 8:26–33).

The physical manifestations of the exorcisms Jesus performed were often dramatic. Shrieking, convulsing, and crying out in recognition of Jesus as *Son of God* or *Holy One of God* are behaviors that accompanied the departure of demons from the possessed (Mark 1:23–26; Luke 4:33–35, 41). On two occasions, the mere sight of Jesus was enough to cause these reactions (Mark 9:20; Luke 8:28). During Jesus' exorcism of the possessed boy, the demon caused him to shout, convulse, and foam at the mouth (Matt. 17:14–18; Mark 9:14–29; Luke 9:37–42).

In other exorcisms recorded in the Gospels, the details vary. Jesus repeatedly forbade demons to speak, especially to say his name (Mark 1:23–26, 34; Luke 4:34–35, 41). During the exorcism of the Gerasene demoniacs, on the other hand, Christ asked the demon its name (Mark 5:9; Luke 8:30). In two Gospels, the number of demons is mentioned: hundreds were driven from the Gerasene demoniacs (Mark 5:9) and seven were expelled from Mary Magdalene (Luke 8:2). There is one instance in which Jesus exorcised a demon even though the possessed child herself was not physically present (Matt. 15:22–28, Mark 7:24–30). On all of the occasions in which Jesus performed exorcisms, it is either implied or stated explicitly that the symptoms of those who were possessed were completely relieved. But Jesus warned that it is possible for an expelled demon to possess its victim again, and in fact to return with other demons, leaving the person in an even worse condition (Matt. 12:43–45).

Jesus said that his followers would drive out demons in his name (Mark 16:17), and the New Testament records that his apostles did so on many occasions. He sent the twelve apostles to visit towns and villages in Israel in order to cure the sick and expel demons, which they were able to do successfully (Matt. 10:1–7; Mark 6:7–13; Luke 9:1–6). He later sent seventy-two followers on a similar mission, and upon their return they reported that Jesus' name gave them power over demons (Luke 10:1, 17–20). This power was also mentioned when a man, not of their company, was said to be driving out demons in Jesus' name. Jesus overruled the objections of his apostles and allowed the man to continue this practice (Mark 9:38–39; Luke 9:49–50).

In the Acts of the Apostles, St. Philip is described as expelling demons from many people in Samaria. When certain Jewish exorcists attempted to drive out demons using the name of Jesus, one demon said it did not recognize them, and the possessed man violently attacked them (Acts 19:13–16). Paul performed an exorcism of a slave girl who was possessed by a clairvoyant spirit, which gave her fortune-telling ability (Acts 16:16–18). The Christians in Ephesus touched cloths to Paul's skin and used them to drive out demons from the sick (Acts 19:11–12).

On one occasion involving a possessed child, the apostles were unable to drive out the demon. When asked why they could not do so, Jesus said that it required strong faith, prayer, and fasting to drive out that demon (Matt. 17:19–21; Mark 9:28–29).

MENTAL DISORDERS VS. DEMONIC POSSESSION

The concept of insanity was familiar to the Israelites during the time of the Old Testament (1 Sam. 21:13–16) and the New Testament (Acts 26:24–25). The inspired writers of these possession stories were not saying that people were possessed when they meant the people were insane—they knew the difference. Moreover, the Gospels distinguish between the exorcisms performed by Jesus and his followers and the miraculous physical healings they accomplished (Matt. 4:24; 10:1; Mark 1:32–34; 6:7–13; Luke 4:40–41; 9:1–6). In the incident at Gerasene, after his exorcism the possessed man was seen to be in his right mind (Mark 5:15). This implies that the man was both mentally ill *and* possessed, and Jesus healed him from both afflictions. The same possibility may be applied to the several reported cases in which physical maladies were caused by demonic activity. The victims may have been suffering from both physical and demonic problems (Matt. 9:32–33; 12:22; Mark 9:14–27; Luke 11:14; 13:10–13).

Based on the descriptions of possession, we can see particular signs that distinguish demonic possession from mental disorders. The possessed Gerasene man showed abnormal physical strength in his ability to break chains, and he seemed to know Jesus' identity as soon as he saw him. These two signs of unnatural strength and knowledge make a good case for demonic possession. Other incidents in the Gospels also describe possessed people having immediate knowledge of Jesus' identity. However, there is little else to distinguish demonic possession from mental disorders.

Therefore, we have just two signs in the Gospels that appear to distinguish demonic possession from mental disorders: the unnatural physical power of the Gerasene demoniac and the inexplicable knowledge of many of the demoniacs that Jesus was the Son of God. Jesus, of course, did not need to witness any signs to know who was possessed, who had mental (or physical) disorders, and who was afflicted by both. However, as we do not have his divine knowledge, we need observable signs.

~

The Old Testament describes particular demonic attacks: tempting human beings to break God's laws, provoking rage and violence, making false accusations, destroying property, causing disease and injury, and committing murder. In the New Testament, we are warned to beware the temptations of the devil. We see the power of demons to possess people, including physical manifestations such as shrieking, convulsing, and throwing the victim to the ground. Demons also cause physical ailments such as weakness, muteness, and the inability to stand straight. They might cause mental disorders, as evidenced by a possessed man who lived amongst tombs, screamed, and gashed himself with stones. Physical powers beyond nature are also shown in that incident, as the man was able to break chains and shackles (Luke 8:27). Demons may manifest knowledge that is hidden from human beings, such as knowledge of who Jesus is; and they may have the ability to predict the future with superhuman accuracy, i.e. fortune telling.

As described in the Gospels, Jesus performed many exorcisms simply by giving a word of command to the demons. Only once did he ask the demon's name. The demons sometimes caused the victim to cry out, shriek, and convulse as they were expelled. The apostles, Paul, and at least one unidentified man performed exorcisms in Jesus' name. People also used sacred objects—particularly, cloths touched by Paul's skin—to drive out demons.

As we will see in the next several chapters, the Catholic Church continues to preserve these biblical teachings and practices regarding demons and exorcism.

3

Catholic Demonology

As we noted earlier, *demonology* means the study of demons. In addition to the Church's teaching on demons, in this chapter we will look at some explanations from St. Thomas Aquinas as well as opinions from Catholic exorcists. I will be careful to point out which statements are the actual teachings of the Magisterium and which are the opinions of experts in the field of demonology.

What Are Demons?

The Catholic Church offers little in the way of official pronouncements that go beyond the biblical texts regarding demons, possession, and exorcism. In the thirteenth century, the Fourth Lateran Council reiterated the belief that the demons were created good by God, but became evil when they sinned of their own free will. This assertion was in response to the *Cathar* or *Albigensian* heresy which held that Satan and the evil spirits are not created by God and are inherently evil. In the sixteenth century, the Catechism of the Council of Trent (part IV, petition 6) repeated the biblical descriptions of the nature and work of demons: they are evil, hateful, powerful, and numerous; they tempt human beings to sin in order to deprive them of heaven. The council went on to state that prayer can be a strong defense against the activity of demons.

The *Catechism of the Catholic Church* (CCC; 391–395) provides other details: it was not a lack of God's mercy, but instead the nature of the demons' evil choice, that rendered them forever evil; they can harm human beings both spiritually and physically; and it is a mystery why God, in his permissive will, allows demons to continue to afflict human beings. The *Catechism* (1673) adds that as Jesus performed exorcisms, so bishops may also appoint priests to do the same through his power.

ST. THOMAS AQUINAS ON DEMONS

Because of his stature as one of the greatest Doctors of the Church, we will again look at what Thomas Aquinas said about demons and their abilities.[20] Demons are forever unhappy, he says, because they want God's creation to be different than it is, and they will never succeed in changing it to their liking. Sometimes they are in hell, and sometimes they are on earth; however, when they are present in the earthly realm, they still suffer the misery of hell:

> Although a heavenly place belongs to the glory of the angels, yet their glory is not lessened by their coming to us, for they consider that place to be their own; in the same way as we say that the bishop's honor is not lessened while he is not actually sitting on his throne. In like manner it must be said, that although the demons are not actually bound within the fire of hell while they are in this dark atmosphere, nevertheless their punishment is none the less; because they know that such confinement is their due. Hence it is said in a gloss upon James 3:6: "They carry fire of hell with them wherever they go."[21]

Demons will always have the intelligence that God gave them when he created them, but since they rebelled against him, he has not given them any more knowledge. Like the good spirits, the evil spirits have the ability to move material objects. They cannot work miracles, which by definition are reserved to God and therefore beyond the ability of any creatures. Still, they may have abilities not known to human beings, and these abilities may fool people into thinking they perform miracles. Demons can also trick our senses, making us think we are seeing and hearing things that aren't really there. But although they can put ideas into our imagination, they cannot read our minds or force our free will decisions.

How Demons Deceive Us

Although the powers of demons are infinitely weaker than the powers of God, they are still greater than those of humans, and their powers can fool us if we are not careful. For example, only God knows all things, including the future. God does not see time in a linear fashion as past, present, and future; rather, he sees all time at once. Everything that ever has been, is now, and ever will be, is present to him at once. Demons, however, exist in time as we do, so they do not know the future. However, they are very intelligent and can make it appear that they know the future. One might think of them as extremely accurate weathermen: they don't know the future, but they can make very good predictions.

Demons also have knowledge of human beings throughout history, and thereby know all human languages, including ancient ones. As we will see later, signs of demon possession include knowledge of things that the possessed individuals could not have known on their own, as well as the ability to speak languages that they have never heard.

Demons have the power to communicate with other demons and with human beings. However, being pure spirits, they communicate in a spiritual rather than a physical way.

As mentioned previously, Aquinas maintained that demons could affect our imagination. This ability does not differ greatly from our powers of communication. We communicate ideas to one another all the time through speaking and writing. Every time we turn on the television, read a newspaper or magazine, or search the Internet, we see advertisements. These are nothing more than someone trying to plant ideas or images in our imagination.

A particularly frightening ability of demons involves how well they know our personal habits. We have only to think of people whom we know very well. When they talk to us, we often know more of what is on their minds than they say, due to hints in their affect: we notice their tone of voice, facial expressions, and body language. Because of demons' greater intelligence, memory, and powers of observation, they are much better at interpreting human behavior and thought than we are. The demons can listen to us and observe us carefully, and may be able to see or hear subtle physical signs that show our emotions. Therefore, even though God alone knows all of our thoughts, demons can readily analyze what we are thinking and feeling, and make accurate predictions.

Demons may thus fool people such as psychics and their clients into thinking that people who are supposedly sensitive to the paranormal can read minds. For example, a demon knows that I am feeling very sad about the recent death of a friend. I go to a psychic, hoping to learn something as to the state of my friend's soul. The demon knows about the death and observes that I am feeling down. He can suggest to the psychic's mind that I am sad over the death of my friend. Although he has never met me, the psychic can tell me how I am feeling and why. We both think the psychic is somehow reading my mind and my feelings, when we are both just being used and deceived by the devil.

Consider another example: by knowing my personal habits and by listening to my conversations today, a demon may foresee some of the things that I will be doing tomorrow. Through his own observations or through communication with another demon, this particular demon may also know the plans of another person. Because of this, the demon may have access to the knowledge that our separate scheduling of appointments will result in our being in the same place at the same time. Now, suppose I were to go to a palm reader today. The demon may suggest to the palm reader's mind the name of the person I am going to meet the next day and the likely circumstances of our encounter. The palm reader thinks he is predicting the future, but instead he is being used by the devil. When the encounter takes place tomorrow, I may think that the palm reader predicted the future, but in reality it was just demonic trickery.

Demons can also deceive us through their ability to move physical objects. An example of telekinesis by a demon can be seen in the book of Job (1:13–19). In that biblical account, the devil caused lightning to kill the shepherds and sheep. In the same story, demons also caused a great wind that destroyed the house of Job's children, thus killing them. The Gospels tell us that demons caused a herd of pigs to run off a cliff, fall into the lake, and drown (Mark 5:1–13).

TEMPTATION

Demonic attacks can be divided into ordinary and extraordinary. We call the ordinary attacks *temptation*. Temptations can come from the world and the flesh, as well as from the devil. Temptations of the world include wealth, popularity, and power; temptations of the flesh include sex, food, and abuse of alcohol and drugs. The temptations of the devils are intertwined with those of the world and the flesh: they give us added encouragement toward those sins (CCC 2846–2854). Temptation by demons is not much different from temptations that come from other people. Demons simply do it without speaking out loud.

All of this can sound frightening, as it should. However, strengthened by God's grace, we have the means to resist these demonic temptations. At the moment of temptation, we can ask for God's help and that of our guardian angel and favorite saints. Taking time to pray every day, receiving Holy Communion and going to confession regularly are ways of building spiritual immunity to the temptations of the demons. The more strongly we practice these spiritual habits, the better we will be at resisting temptations from the devil and his demons.

Oppression and Obsession

Exorcists often speak about demonic attacks that fall somewhere in between the categories of temptation and possession. These types of attacks are not part of Church teaching; rather, they are acceptable Catholic opinions. In the Bible, we can see the basis for this level of demonic attack. For example, the devil did not possess Job (1:13–2:7), but instead caused the death of his children, triggered murderous attacks and plundering by his enemies, and gave Job a painful skin disease. When Jesus saw a woman who was permanently bent over due to a "spirit of infirmity," he laid his hands on her and cured her (Luke 13:10–16). Jesus said the woman had been "bound" by Satan, but the Gospel does not say she was possessed; furthermore, Jesus did not address the demon directly. This woman did not display the signs of possession that are recorded elsewhere in the Gospels, such as demons shrieking at the sight of Jesus and screaming his name. Therefore, it is possible that she was suffering from a demonic attack that was less than full-fledged possession.

The two types of attacks that fall into this category are usually called *oppression* and *obsession*. Demonic oppression is often described as an attack that is external in some way. Again, the biblical accounts of Job and the woman with the spirit of infirmity are good examples of the ways in which demons may attack people physically without possessing them. Some exorcists say that in addition to causing physical diseases, demonic oppression may involve attacks on the victims' finances, relationships, and employment. In Job's case, we believe it to be a demonic attack because the biblical account records it as being demonic. However, outside of the Bible it would be practically impossible to discern this type of attack.

Demonic *obsession* usually refers to an attack that is internal in some way. Exorcists note that the characteristics of internal attacks associated with demonic obsession include evil thoughts that victims cannot stop, spirits that cling to emotional wounds or unhealthy relationships, and evil or frightening dreams. As a counselor, I have talked to people struggling with drug and alcohol addictions who describe their addictive behaviors as demonic. I have met young women with anorexia who described an evil voice that told them they deserved to starve and suffer as punishment for the problems they caused their families. Among the many people I have met who suffer from audial and visual hallucinations, seeing and hearing demons is common.

All of these problems are demonic in a certain way, since Satan is the primary cause of evil in the world, and his demons are always looking for ways to inflict damage on us. However, it would be a mistake to give the devil too much credit for such problems. Demons can play a role in physical illnesses, but we should always look for physical causes and medical cures. Common sense dictates that healthcare professionals and counselors should be included in the evaluation and treatment of patients who suffer from physical, emotional, and mental problems. The bottom line is that because demons are evil and cruel, they attack all of us at our weak points.

POSSESSION

In conformity with the words of Jesus (Matt. 17:18–19, Mark 1:23–26), the Catholic Rite of Exorcism refers to demons being *in* possessed persons and the process of exorcism as driving the demons *out* of persons. Now, demons are purely spiritual beings, and therefore do not occupy space as do material objects (CCC 330). The manner in which demons are *in* or *out* of persons (or places) is a matter of philosophical and theological debate. When it comes to possession and exorcism, though, the important factor is that demons are exerting their power over the bodies of the possessed. The demons are literally *in possession* of the victims' bodies, and are therefore controlling their words and actions.

Movies sometimes show possession as demons trying to drag people's souls to hell. This is not at all what possession means. Demons cannot literally drag our bodies or souls into hell. What they hope to do, through temptation, is to make us hardened sinners who are not sorry for our sins— thereby leading us on the path to hell.

HOW DO PEOPLE BECOME POSSESSED BY DEMONS?

Exorcists are in general agreement as to how a person becomes possessed by demons. As one exorcist says, "The darkness is there, waiting to receive an invitation."[22]

Exorcists identify three categories of activities and experiences that open a person to demonic possession. We can think of these categories as doors for demonic attacks: they invite demons in, but they do not always result in possession. In fact, as we shall see, full-fledged demonic possession may be extremely rare—depending upon whose opinion we accept.

The first category is referred to as *patterns of sin*. This does not mean simply being a sinner, since all of us are sinners. Rather, this refers to people who have a habit of serious sin that they like, are attached to, and have no desire or intention of stopping. There is a conscious decision to give one's self over to the sin. Demons can see this as an invitation to their activity.

The second category of influences that invite demons into one's life is *the occult*. Occult practices include Satanism, the use of tarot cards and the Ouija board, and consulting psychics and mediums. This also includes necromancy, the attempt to consult with spirits of the dead for the sake of learning hidden knowledge or future events.

Being a victim of *trauma or abuse* is a third category of experience that can open the door to demonic possession. The trauma may be witnessing a murder, suicide, or horrific accident; the abuse may be sexual, physical, or psychological. One exorcist explains that those who go through these experiences can end up living in the dark emotions of anger, rage, resentment, and revenge.[23] He stressed the importance of such victims getting the psychological and spiritual help that they need, in order to have some degree of healing. If they do not, those emotions can weaken their relationship with God, and simultaneously be an opening to a relationship with evil spirits.

Magic, Evil Signs, and Instruments

According to the Rite of Exorcism, the exorcist should command demons to reveal whether they are held or detained in the possessed individual by means of *magicam, aut malefica signa, vel instrumenta.* English versions of the rite usually translate this phrase as *necromancy, or evil signs, or amulets,* though the word *magicam* may also be translated as *magic.* In regard to the *malefica instrumenta,* an *evil instrument* or *amulet,* the exorcist should order the possessed individual to reveal any cursed objects he may have concealed on (or *in,* if swallowed) his person. An object that is cursed in some way is not inherently evil, but the devil might be more likely to use it for his evil purposes.

The rite instructs exorcists to burn such objects. In regard to objects that do not burn (such as medallions or stone images), one exorcist advised that they be smashed, if possible, then either buried or discarded in a body of water. Another suggested that they be defaced in such a way that the original semblance is damaged, sprinkled with holy water, and then simply disposed of. The latter exorcist emphasized that it is important not to be overly concerned about the treatment of such objects, and not to attribute to them more power than they actually possess.

Is it truly possible for someone to cause others to be possessed through the use of magic, spells, or curses? In a certain sense the answer is no, because a human being cannot force demons to possess another person. On the other hand, demons may cooperate with evil people, and it is possible for them to possess individuals at the request of such evildoers.

DEMONIC INFESTATION AND HAUNTED HOUSES

Infestation means that demons are exerting their power over a particular place, or something other than a human being. The Rite of Exorcism has a set of prayers that is specifically intended for cases of infestation. Officially titled the *Exorcism of Satan and the Fallen Angels,* the rite is sometimes also called the *Prayers of Leo XIII* (Leo being the pope who added these prayers to the rite). The 1999 Rite of Exorcism contains prayers for this purpose in an appendix entitled, *A Supplication and Exorcism which May be Used in Particular Circumstances of the Church*.[24]

The only clear case of demonic infestation in the Bible is the incident involving the possessed Gerasene man (Matt. 8:26–34; Mark 5:1–20; Luke 8:26–39). When Jesus drove the demons from the man, our Lord allowed them to enter into a herd of pigs. The demonic control of animals, therefore, is one type of infestation. Another type is when demons attack a specific city or community. Probably the most well-known type of infestation is when demons cause a disturbance in a particular place such as a house or other building. It is common to say that a place is *haunted*.

If we keep in mind Catholic doctrine, we can narrow the possible explanations for haunted houses. In regard to animals, there are no animal souls in heaven, hell, or purgatory for the simple reason that they do not have immortal souls. There is nothing left of them when they die. Another way to look at it is that Jesus died for human beings, not animals. Since there are no souls of terriers, tarantulas, or tuna in the afterlife, we can rule out the possibility of houses being haunted by them.

People often think of haunted houses as being inhabited by the spirits of dead human beings. We must remember that the souls of the dead are either in heaven, hell, or purgatory. The saints in heaven can speak to people if God wills it, but there is no reason for them to cause mischief in a house or other building. The same can be said of the souls in purgatory, or the *poor souls* as they are sometimes called. The only reason for souls to be in purgatory is to undergo suffering in order to be purified of the sins they committed during their lives on earth. The Bible says that we can help the poor souls make retribution for their sins by offering prayers and sacrifices for them (2 Macc. 12:32–46). It is possible that the poor souls may somehow be doing their penance by helping people in this world, or that they may appear to people to ask that prayers and sacrifices be offered for them. However, it is difficult to see how the poor souls would be purified for heaven by making noises, flickering lights, and moving objects around a house.

That leaves us with demons and the souls of the dead in hell. The Church does not have a definitive teaching as to whether the souls of the damned can haunt a place. What is certain is that demons *can* cause the things we commonly associate with haunted houses. They can make noises and move objects; they can trigger air movements, such as a breeze; and they can cause the temperature in a room to drop. Demons can appear in the form of human beings, including someone who once lived in the haunted house, or even our own family members and friends.[25] They may also appear in the form of animals, as was described in the case of a house haunted by the spirit of what appeared to be the recently euthanized cat.[26]

Why would a demon haunt a house? The answer is simple: demons will resort to any means possible to persuade people to focus on ghosts and hauntings rather than on God. Consider our culture's high level of interest in books, shows, and movies that deal with demonic infestation. By getting people to focus on meaningless spiritual diversions such as haunted houses, the demons hope to distract them from truly important spiritual realities such as sin and the state of their own souls.

~

We have surveyed different cultures' beliefs regarding the interaction between spirits and human beings, and we have looked at the teachings of the Church on the nature of demons and their assaults on the human race. As the purpose of this book is to identify the differences between demonic activity and mental disorders, we will begin to describe how this is done, especially by Catholic exorcists. The first step will be to consider mental disorders that may be similar in appearance to demonic problems.

4

Demonic Attack or Mental Disorder?

We have seen that demons are purely spiritual, purely malicious beings that frequently tempt us to sin. Less frequently, they may attack us externally by causing physical illnesses or relationship problems, or internally through hallucinations, nightmares, and negative thoughts. Demons may also exert their influence on particular places or objects, thereby causing problems for people in contact with the place or object. The most dramatic and frightening type of demonic attack—and the least common—is possession, or taking control of a person's body.

Some indications of these demonic attacks correspond with symptoms of mental and emotional disorders. For example, relationship problems may be the result of personality disorders, hallucinations are associated with schizophrenia, and nightmares can be caused by post-traumatic stress. In this chapter, we look at mental disorders that can have effects similar to demonic assaults.

The Rite of Exorcism lists three signs that may accompany demon possession: speaking or understanding a formerly unknown language, infused knowledge of future or hidden events, and the manifestation of physical powers outside of nature. It also suggests a fourth sign: a negative reaction to the sacred. For now, it is crucial to keep in mind that *the three signs of demonic possession given in the Rite of Exorcism are, for the most part, different from the symptoms of any mental disorder.* When exorcists speculate about other signs that might indicate demonic possession,[27] they risk confusing possession with mental disorders.

What are the costs and benefits of this risk? One cost is that mental problems can be aggravated by calling them demonic attacks and treating them accordingly. The last thing a mentally or emotionally disturbed person needs is to be told—erroneously—that he has the devil inside him. Another cost is that the Church may face ridicule if its members, particularly priests, purport to see demons where there are none. On the other hand, the reality of demonic attacks cannot be ignored by the Church. Doing so would consign those so afflicted to suffering that could be relieved by the proper spiritual help. Exorcists can best balance this question by being familiar with the diagnosis of mental disorders, or by consulting someone who is.

Of course, it is possible for individuals to be suffering from both demonic possession and mental disorders simultaneously. In fact, one exorcist says that practically all the cases of possession he has seen have involved individuals who also suffered from mental disorders.[28] This is actually quite reasonable, according to the evil logic of the devil. Consider the idea of a bully who tries to make life miserable for people who are unable to defend themselves. Demons are the ultimate bullies, so who better to torment than those who are already suffering from mental disorders?

CHEMICAL IMBALANCE THEORY

When talking about mental and emotional problems, it is common to use the phrase *mental illness.* Sometimes, in conversation, we hear it said that a mental illness is just like physical illness—and indeed, there are some ways in which mental and physical illness are alike. They can both involve genetic predisposition toward particular conditions, diagnosis by a standardized set of symptoms, and treatment involving medication. However, mental and physical illnesses also differ in important ways. Many mental illnesses can be improved or even cured by psychological or spiritual counseling. They often do not have a physical cause such as bacteria, a virus, or a tumor, and they cannot be diagnosed with a blood test. Because of such differences, I prefer the term mental *disorder* rather than mental *illness*. It would be helpful to use the term mental illness, consequently, in referencing those conditions where the physical cause can be pinpointed: such as a head injury, brain tumor, or a disease such as encephalitis. The majority of mental problems do not result from physical causes such as these.

There is a common popular belief that most or all mental problems are caused by "chemical imbalances." However, this concept is unsubstantiated, no closer to being proved today than it was over 2,000 years ago when the ancient Greeks had the idea that psychiatric disorders were caused by an imbalance of four bodily fluids called *humors*.[29] Instead of relying upon the humors paradigm, today's chemical imbalance theory of mental illness is largely based on whether a patient has proper levels of brain chemicals such as dopamine, serotonin, and norepinephrine. Yet there is no blood test, spinal tap, or other means of gauging an individual's neurochemistry, determining which chemical or chemicals are at the root of a particular mental disorder, or providing the precise dosage of medicine to remedy the imbalance. That is why psychiatrists often must use trial and error in determining medications and appropriate dosages for patients, and why sometimes psychiatrists are unable to find *any* medicine that helps.

There certainly are some mental problems that can be directly linked to brain chemistry, and therefore can be improved or cured by chemical means. One of the most serious of these is post-partum depression, which in severe cases can include psychosis, delusion, and suicidal impulses. Tragically, there have been highly publicized cases where mothers suffering from this have killed themselves and/or their children. Another example is a malfunctioning thyroid gland. An overactive thyroid gland (hyperthyroidism) can cause anxiety and nervousness, whereas a poorly functioning thyroid (hypothyroidism) can result in symptoms of depression. Physical symptoms such as weight changes also typically accompany these conditions. A third example is a deficiency in electrolytes, such as potassium. I have seen this a number of times, often among older patients who were dehydrated. When dehydration occurs, patients may decline rapidly from being mentally sharp and alert to being very confused.

These examples show that mental disorders are sometimes the result of chemical imbalances. We should not rule out the possibility that additional disorders may result from such imbalances. However, we cannot logically conclude that because some mental disorders are caused by chemical imbalances, that all mental disorders share this same cause.

DIAGNOSING MENTAL DISORDERS

The Diagnostic and Statistical Manual of Mental Disorders—Fifth Edition[30] (DSM–5), published by the American Psychiatric Association (APA), has categories of disorders, specific disorders carefully identified within each category, and a list of symptoms that are common to each disorder. Although the DSM–5 is written by and for psychiatrists, it is also the diagnostic book used in the United States by all licensed psychologists, counselors, and social workers.

As the title of the DSM implies, its purpose is not to give the causes or cures of mental disorders, but to *diagnose* them.

Accurate diagnosis—or definition, we could say—helps mental health professionals in two ways. First, when talking to one another, they are all using the same terms. The second value of a diagnosis is for treatment. As a counselor I don't have to reinvent the wheel. I can read about a disorder and talk to other professionals to learn what approaches have been most helpful.

Dissociative Identity Disorder[31]

Those in the over-forty age group may remember the book and TV mini-series from the mid-1970s called *Sybil*.[32] It was publicized as the true story of a young woman whose childhood traumas led her to develop sixteen different personalities. The story, however, is controversial.[33] Sybil's therapy may have involved hypnosis and use of the drug amobarbital, both of which can result in false memories. Some allege that the psychiatrist in the case deliberately tried to elicit the different personalities, and that Sybil simply went along with the psychiatrist's covert suggestions. The book's author and Sybil's psychiatrist have been accused of fabricating some of the stories for the sake of selling the book and movie. (In their defense, however, the same accusation has been made about the author of one of the books critical of Sybil's psychiatrist.)[34]

One thing is certain: the diagnosis of multiple personality disorder, which has since been renamed dissociative identity disorder (DID), remains controversial. One theory rejects the notion of individuals having completely separate identities. This theory agrees that those diagnosed with DID are suffering from some kind of mental disorder, often caused by abuse and trauma. They may have read about DID, seen movies such as *Sybil*, and/or have therapists who explain it to them (either explicitly or implicitly). These individuals see DID as a reasonable explanation for their disorder, and are simply following the role that is expected of them. This theory may explain why there was a dramatic increase in people diagnosed with the disorder after the movie *Sybil* was seen by millions of people in 1976.[35] I have met people with DID, and they seem to be surprisingly perceptive and knowledgeable regarding the disorder in general and their own different identities in particular.

The standard theory is that DID is caused by trauma, especially childhood physical and sexual abuse. Painful thoughts and feelings connected to the trauma are then linked to imaginary friends, fanciful creations of the mind that are common among children. During highly stressful situations, the imaginary friends become more prominent and may function in place of the self. The child begins to *dissociate*, which means that he is experiencing the start of separate personalities or identities. During adolescence, the imaginary friends complete the split from self and develop their own personalities or identities.

The identities, often called *alters*, develop as needed in response to the abuse and the emotions that go along with it. For example, shame may result in an alter that is weak and allows itself to be hurt; anger may produce one that seeks revenge and is hostile; fear may create an alter that is protective. The alter most closely associated with an individual's original identity is called the *host*. Alters are usually aware of at least some of their fellow alters and of the host. The host often does not realize when a transition takes place between one identity and another. Months or years may pass with another identity in control while the host is not conscious of it.

Some alters are described as frightening and violent. Their negative behaviors may include self-mutilation, suicide, violence, and murder.[36]

What does all of this have to do with demon possession? The answer depends upon the particular exorcist's approach.

For now, we will note the aspects of DID that sound like some exorcists' beliefs regarding demon possession:

- A primary characteristic of DID is the presence of two or more identities or personality states that recurrently control behavior. In cases of possession, some exorcists describe a second personality that emerges during the process of the exorcism, and often outside of it as well. Some exorcists talk about numerous personalities that they believe correspond to different demonic spirits.
- One requirement for individuals to be diagnosed with DID is that they repeatedly forget important information and events that people would normally remember. When one alter is in control, it might not remember what the other alters did, and it may not even know that other alters exist. The individuals may not know they have DID, and instead think of it as blackouts lasting for days, months, or years. This is also typical in cases of possession: individuals often don't remember time periods when the evil personality was present, which may occur during periods of crisis and/or during the exorcism ceremony. These are usually shorter periods of time such as hours or days, but some exorcists say they have seen cases where this continues for weeks or months.
- Significant distress and/or impairment in functioning is a part of DID; it is also described by some exorcists in cases of possession.
- Facial contortions and eyes rolling back are descriptions of DID patients switching from one alternate identity to another[37] and also of possessed persons, especially during periods of crisis and exorcism.
- The commonly held theory of DID states that it results from childhood abuse or other trauma. Similarly, being a

victim of abuse or another trauma may also open the door to demonic possession.

- People with DID sometimes speak with different-sounding voices, depending upon which alter is in control. Similarly, alleged cases of demon possession sometimes include victims speaking in voices unlike their normal voice. Some exorcists take these different voices to be different demons manifesting their presence. However, it is important to note that this is not the same as the first sign given in the Rite of Exorcism—facility in a strange language. For this sign to be fulfilled, it is not enough for possessed individuals to speak with a different tone, pitch, or accent. Rather, it requires that he speak or understand a language that he has no way of knowing.

Schizophrenia Spectrum and Other Psychotic Disorders[38]

The word *schizophrenic* is commonly used to describe a person who exhibits contradictory or rapidly shifting attitudes or moods. The clinical description is somewhat different: individuals with *schizophrenia* are out of touch with reality in some way. There are several diagnoses that together make up the schizophrenia spectrum. Brief psychotic disorder takes place when schizophrenic symptoms last for less than one month; schizophreniform disorder occurs when the symptoms continue for one to six months; and schizophrenia is present when the symptoms of the ailment exist for more than six months.

The diagnosis for these disorders requires that individuals have serious problems functioning in areas such as work, school, personal relationships, or self-care. Furthermore, patients must show at least two additional symptoms. Some exorcists consider these symptoms to be potential signs of demon possession, but the symptoms do not coincide with the three signs given in the Rite of Exorcism. The additional symptoms are:

- *Delusions, which are related to thoughts*: these are beliefs that individuals hold even when they are proven false. For example, patients may think that CIA agents are following them, or that a celebrity is in love with them, or that their internal organs were secretly removed.
- *Hallucinations, which are related to the senses:* these are vivid perceptions of things that are not there. For example, they may hear voices that are not real, or see people who are not present.
- *Disorganized speech:* individuals may abruptly and frequently switch from one topic to another in conversations, give irrelevant responses, or provide nonsensical answers to questions.
- *Grossly disorganized behavior:* this manifests itself in a pattern of excessively child-like or unpredictable actions. Patients can also exhibit catatonic behavior, in which they seem to ignore what is going on around them.
- *Negative symptoms:* these can include showing little to no emotion, eye contact, or body language, sitting and doing nothing for long periods of time, or exhibiting no motivation to do purposeful activity.

There are a few more diagnoses in this category whose symptoms are similar to those sometimes reported of possessed individuals. People with delusional disorder behave and function normally, with the exception of one persistent delusion. Schizoaffective disorder is practically the same as the schizophrenia spectrum, with the addition of a depressive or manic episode. In the appendix of DSM–5, in the section titled *Conditions for Further Study*, there is a disorder called attenuated psychosis syndrome.[39] This is similar to the schizophrenia spectrum disorders, but is not as severe; the individuals are more in touch with reality.

There is one delusional symptom of schizophrenia spectrum disorders that may coincide with demonic possession. Some individuals believe that their body is being controlled by an outside force, such as an alien or an evil spirit.[40] Individuals who are actually possessed by demons may have the same belief. However, this belief itself is not one of the signs of demonic possession. Rather than relying on the subject's belief or feeling of having lost control, the Rite of Exorcism provides signs that can be observed by others.

As chaplain of a hospital with an inpatient mental health unit, I frequently visit people suffering from some type of schizophrenia. In my experience, it is somewhat rare for them to feel or believe demons are controlling their bodies. More commonly, they claim to hear or see demons, or attribute mysterious incidents (such as inexplicably moving objects) to demonic activity. Although any one of these instances could be truly demonic, I presume that this is rare. Supporting my presumption is that the feelings and beliefs dissipate as the person's mental condition improves. Clearly, we do not want to accept as objectively valid every feeling or belief that an evil spirit is controlling someone's body.

DEPRESSIVE DISORDERS[41]

There are a number of disorders in this category that are popularly known as *depression*. A major depressive episode is characterized by a number of symptoms that are also reported in cases of possession; however, none of these corresponds with the three signs found in the rite. The symptoms are:

- depressed mood, diminished interest or pleasure in activities,
- insomnia or hypersomnia (excessive sleep), loss of energy,
- feelings of worthlessness or guilt,
- inability to think or concentrate,
- recurrent thoughts of death or suicide.

SOMATIC SYMPTOMS AND RELATED DISORDERS[42]

Somatic symptoms and related disorders make up a complicated category of mental disorders. In fact, it is a drastic revision of a category called somatoform disorders in the previous edition of the DSM.[43] It is enough for our purposes to know that these disorders sometimes involve complaints involving physical symptoms for which doctors cannot find a sufficient cause. These symptoms, which may continue for years, include bodily pain, gastrointestinal problems, and neurological disorders. Again, although these somatic complaints are not the same as the three signs of possession in the Rite of Exorcism, some exorcists consider them to be signs.

REACTION TO SACRED WORDS AND OBJECTS

The Rite of Exorcism instructs exorcists to use particular prayers and objects including a crucifix, holy water, and relics of saints. Exorcists are unanimous in stating that the most common and dominant sign of possession is revulsion to these sacred words and objects. Although such behavior is not part of any DSM diagnosis, a negative reaction to religious themes may be an aspect of mental disorders that involve paranoia.[44] For example, individuals may believe they are being followed or otherwise persecuted by members of a mysterious religious group, or they may believe the Vatican is secretly in charge of the American government. These individuals may react negatively to religious symbols. Individuals who have been abused by clergy or others wearing identifiably religious garb or symbols may also react negatively when they later see these same clothes or symbols.

My personal observations of psychotic individuals are quite different. For over ten years, I have regularly visited people who are in the psychiatric units of hospitals. It is not unusual for those with psychotic symptoms to talk frequently about Satan, to see or hear devils, and to believe that demons are moving objects or causing other disturbances. However, rather than a negative reaction to the sacred, I see the opposite. These individuals commonly ask me to say a prayer for them, and this often has a calming effect, at least for a little while. Also, I have sprinkled holy water on hundreds of such patients, and have never seen anyone exhibit a negative reaction.

HISTORICAL NOTE REGARDING THE CHURCH

In dealing with this topic, it appears to be standard practice for authors of secular books to condemn the Church in regard to the historical treatment of the insane.[45] Although I have no doubt that there were abuses, they were just that: abuses.[46] On the whole, the Church's record in treating the mentally ill is laudable. Throughout the Middle Ages, the Church canonized numerous saints—Erhard of Regensburg, John of Matha, Elizabeth of Hungary, Bridget of Sweden, John of God, Camillus de Lellis, and Vincent DePaul, to name but a few—based on their compassion and charity toward the physically and mentally ill.[47] Religious orders were established by some of these saints and sanctioned by the Church for the same purpose. A fair appraisal of the treatment of the mentally ill must contain not only the abuses, but also the practices held as model therapies.

~

Although the DSM–5 can be useful for matters of treatment of mental and emotional problems, it does not attempt to identify causes. In fact, the cause of most mental disorders is uncertain. Whereas head injuries, brain and neurological diseases, and substance abuse are physically identifiable causes of some mental problems, the precise nature of many others is a mystery. The theory that chemical imbalances in the brain are to blame is unproven.

Demons are capable of causing physical and mental harm, but Catholics in general and exorcists in particular should not presume that demons are the sole or primary cause of mental disorders. Doing so can exacerbate such problems, and may also (intentionally or not) deprive individuals of therapy and medication that could be helpful. The Rite of Exorcism, which we will examine next, supports the notion that exorcists should see particular signs before judging a person to be demonically possessed rather than mentally disturbed.

5

The Rite of Exorcism

The Catholic exorcism ceremony, called the *Rite of Exorcism,* was first promulgated in 1614. Although a new rite was promulgated in 1999, the exorcists with whom I have spoken—as well as those whose books I have read—all use the 1614 rite. Therefore, unless otherwise noted, this chapter and the remainder of this book will be referring to the ancient rite rather than the modern.

Exorcists give various reasons for not using the newer version. One said he preferred the rite of 1614 because the exorcist who trained him used it, and therefore he is familiar with it. He also appreciates the fact that it was developed over time through the lived practice of exorcists, whereas the newer rite was written by a committee of theologians in their offices. Others point out that it has already been revised, claim that the prayers are not as authoritative and commanding toward the demons, or just note that it can be difficult to obtain a copy. Another practical reason for using the more ancient rite is its availability in English, which is helpful to exorcists who are not proficient in Latin.[48]

However, as one exorcist explained, it makes no difference to the demons which translation is used. He relates a story from another exorcist who had attempted to use the new rite. The demons responded by saying, "You aren't going to try to get rid of me with *that* translation, are you?" When told this story, the first exorcist responded, "If the devil is the father of lies [John 8:44], why would you believe anything some demon would say to you anyway?"

SACRAMENTS AND SACRAMENTALS

Catholics believe that Jesus Christ established his Church and built it on the apostles, with St. Peter as their head. Christ gave to the Church the power and authority to bestow his grace on individuals through sacred signs called sacraments: "The sacraments, instituted by Christ and entrusted to the Church, are efficacious signs of grace perceptible to the senses. Through them divine life is bestowed upon us."[49] Sacraments work *ex opere operato*, which may be translated *by the work done*. This means that when a sacrament is celebrated according to the ritual of the Church, its intended effect is not dependent upon the person administering it. For example, when people go to confession, if they confess their sins honestly and sincerely ask forgiveness, their sins are forgiven when the priest says the proper words from the Rite of Penance. The priest may be a great saint or a great sinner, but that does not affect the power of the sacrament. The sins of the penitent are forgiven *ex opere operato* by the penitential rite administered by the priest.

There are lesser rituals of the Church called sacramentals, which are defined as "sacred signs instituted by the Church to sanctify different circumstances of life. They include a prayer accompanied by the sign of the cross and other signs."[50] Examples of sacramentals are blessings, holy water, and blessed objects such as crucifixes and rosaries. Sacramentals work in two ways: *ex opere operantis* and *praesertim operante Ecclesia,* which mean *by the work of the doer* and *especially working through the Church*. This means that in some way a sacramental receives its power from the Church, but its effect also depends upon the person doing the work. For example, because of the power the Church gives to a priest, there is a certain spiritual benefit in receiving a blessing from him. However, the power of a blessing or a prayer is also dependent upon the goodness or holiness of the priest or person offering it (James 5:16).

Exorcism is a sacramental, which tells us two things. First, though it may be the Church's most powerful means of expelling demons, in the overall picture it is not as powerful as a sacrament. An exorcism does not forgive a person's mortal sins as the sacrament of penance does; so even though the Rite of Exorcism can drive out demons, it cannot help save souls in the way that a sacrament can.

Furthermore, the power of the exorcism rite comes from the Church, but also depends upon the particular exorcist. An authorized exorcist who properly performs the Rite of Exorcism is going to have some power over demons. However, an exorcist may negate this power if his soul is in a state of mortal sin.[51] That is why the rite instructs bishops to carefully choose virtuous priests to be exorcists. A holier priest will have more power over demons. Of course, the closer that anyone is to Christ, the greater will be his power over demons. The exorcist simply has an additional weapon to use—the Rite of Exorcism.

Definition of Exorcism

The word *exorcism* comes from the Greek word *exorkizo*, which means *to adjure*, which in turn can be defined as *to charge, bind, or command earnestly and solemnly*. The *Catechism* (1673) includes one paragraph on the topic:

> When the Church asks publicly and authoritatively in the name of Jesus Christ that a person or object be protected against the power of the Evil One and withdrawn from his dominion, it is called exorcism. Jesus performed exorcisms and from him the Church has received the power

and office of exorcizing. In a simple form, exorcism is performed at the celebration of Baptism. The solemn exorcism, called "a major exorcism," can be performed only by a priest and with the permission of the bishop. The priest must proceed with prudence, strictly observing the rules established by the Church. Exorcism is directed at the expulsion of demons or to the liberation from demonic possession through the spiritual authority which Jesus entrusted to his Church. Illness, especially psychological illness, is a very different matter; treating this is the concern of medical science. Therefore, before an exorcism is performed, it is important to ascertain that one is dealing with the presence of the Evil One, and not an illness.

In this passage, several meanings of the word *exorcism* appear. An exorcism is the act of driving out demons. It is the name of the solemn ritual. Furthermore, exorcism refers to the specific passages of the rites of baptism and exorcism where the demons are ordered to depart. It is this third meaning—the command addressed to the demons—that is the traditional sense of the word *exorcism*. We see this in the Gospels when Jesus performed exorcisms:

And immediately there was in their synagogue a man with an unclean spirit; and he cried out, "What have you to do with us, Jesus of Nazareth? Have you come to destroy us? I know who you are, the Holy One of God." But Jesus rebuked him, saying, "Be silent, and come out of him!" And the unclean spirit, convulsing him and crying with a loud voice, came out of him. And they were all amazed, so that they questioned among themselves, saying, "What is this? A new teaching! With authority he

commands even the unclean spirits, and they obey him."
(Mark 1:23–17)

Similarly, when St. Paul drives an evil spirit from a young
girl, he commands the demon in the name of Jesus:

> As we were going to the place of prayer, we were met by
> a slave girl who had a spirit of divination and brought her
> owners much gain by soothsaying. She followed Paul and
> us, crying, "These men are servants of the Most High
> God, who proclaim to you the way of salvation." And
> this she did for many days. But Paul was annoyed, and
> turned and said to the spirit, "I charge you in the name
> of Jesus Christ to come out of her." And it came out that
> very hour. (Acts 16:16–18)

The Catholic rites of baptism and exorcism similarly
command the demons to depart. The rites also ask God
for protection against demons, but to be precise those are
prayers, not exorcisms in the traditional sense of the word.
The rites themselves use the word *exorcism* in reference to
the sections in which the demons are commanded to depart.
The exorcism ceremony includes three specific exorcisms—
three occasions in which the priest, in the name of God,
specifically commands the demons to depart. Prior to those
exorcisms, there is a section in which the rubrics direct the
exorcist to command the demons to tell him their names
and the time of their departure.

EXORCISMS IN THE RITE OF BAPTISM

First we will take a brief look at the exorcisms in the Rite
of Baptism. The *Catechism* refers to these as simple or minor

exorcisms, while those in the exorcism ritual are called solemn or major exorcisms (1673). In the modern rite, the priest or deacon mentions the devil but does not speak to him directly. The ancient ritual contains three specific exorcisms—commands directly addressing the devil. The following is an example:

> I cast you out, unclean spirit, in the name of the Father, and of the Son, and of the Holy Spirit. Depart and stay far away from this servant of God, (name). For it is the Lord himself who commands you, accursed and doomed spirit, He who walked on the sea and reached out his hand to Peter as he was sinking. So then, foul fiend, recall the curse that decided your fate once for all. Indeed, pay homage to the living and true God, pay homage to Jesus Christ, his Son, and to the Holy Spirit. Keep far from this servant of God, (name), for Jesus Christ, our Lord and God, has freely called him (her) to his holy grace and blessed way and to the waters of baptism.

In blessing the water and salt used in the rites of baptism and exorcism, the priest addresses these elements as he drives demons out of them: "God's creature, water, I cast out the demon from you in the name of God the Father almighty, in the name of Jesus Christ, His Son, our Lord, and in the power of the Holy Spirit," and, "God's creature, salt, I cast out the demon from you by the living God, by the true God, by the holy God."

OUR PRAYERS OF PROTECTION AGAINST DEMONS

The Church does not teach that using the Rite of Exorcism (and baptism) is the only way to drive demons out of persons,

places, or things. Although only appointed exorcists should use
the rite, anyone can say prayers asking God for protection from
demons, or asking that they be driven out of someone. We
can compare this to the sacrament of anointing of the sick, in
which prayers are said for God's grace and for the cure of those
who are seriously ill. Although only priests are authorized to
administer this sacrament, anyone may pray for the cure of a
sick person, and God answers those prayers as he wills. Just as
we should pray for the sick regularly, we should also pray often
for protection from demons—for ourselves and others.

Why does the Church only allow authorized priests to
use the Rite of Exorcism? For most of Church history, there
were few restrictions on who could perform exorcisms or
how they should be conducted. But lack of oversight meant
that exorcism sometimes looked more like a circus than
a Church ritual. Over time, the Church formalized the
process and restricted who could perform the rite.[52] As we
noted above, the purpose and value of the Rite of Exorcism
is that the priest authorized to use it is not acting on his own,
but has the power of the Church at work through him.

Some Catholics have their own prayers that they believe
are powerful in driving out demons, but we are certainly on
solid ground if we use the prayers provided by the Church.
In the Rite of Exorcism, the exorcist is encouraged to pray
the Our Father, the Hail Mary, and the Athanasian Creed.
Every time we pray the Our Father and ask God to *deliver
us from evil*, we are asking for protection from the devil. Every time we pray the Hail Mary, we invoke the intercession
of the devil's most powerful human foe after Jesus himself.
Every time we pray the Creed, we are affirming our faith
in Jesus Christ and our belief in his teachings, much to the
dread of the demons. Another prayer from the rite that we
can use (in its shortened form) is the Prayer to St. Michael

the Archangel, in which we explicitly ask Michael to send the demons back where they belong: *Do thou, O Prince of the heavenly host, by the divine power of God, cast into hell Satan and all the evil spirits, who roam throughout the world seeking the ruin of souls.* The newer Rite of Exorcism includes an appendix of prayers and invocations that all the faithful may use when experiencing assaults by the devil. In their explanation of the English translation, the American bishops indicate that pastoral counseling, spiritual direction, and the sacrament of penance are possible means of discerning such attacks.[53]

THE RITE OF EXORCISM

The sacraments of the Catholic Church were established by Jesus Christ. This can be seen in the words of the liturgies used for the sacraments. For example, Jesus said "This is my body, this is my blood" at the Last Supper, and the same words are still said by priests to change bread and wine into his body, blood, soul, and divinity at Mass. Jesus told his apostles to baptize "In the name of the Father, and of the Son, and of the Holy Spirit," and these words are still said in the baptism ritual. The words that exorcists use in driving out demons are also found in the Gospels. Jesus commanded the demons possessing the Gerasene man, "Unclean spirit, come out of the man." The Rite of Exorcism uses essentially the same words: "I cast you out, unclean spirit . . . in the name of our Lord Jesus Christ."

The Rite of Exorcism was first promulgated—published for use in the Church—by Pope Paul V in 1614. It has three parts that exorcists often refer to as chapters: the Instructions, the Exorcism of One Possessed by a Demon, and the Exorcism of Satan and the Fallen Angels. I will include excerpts here, with the section numbers found in the Rite of Exorcism.

Chapter I: Instructions

I have not included every section in the Instructions. As can be seen by the numbering, I have rearranged some of the sections in order to fit them to our purposes:

1. A priest—one who is expressly and particularly authorized by the ordinary—when he intends to perform an exorcism over persons tormented by the devil, must be properly distinguished for his piety, prudence, and integrity of life. He should fulfill this devout undertaking in all constancy and humility, being utterly immune to any striving for human aggrandizement, and relying, not on his own, but on the divine power. Moreover, he ought to be of mature years, and revered not alone for his office but for his moral qualities.

2. In order to exercise his ministry rightly, he should resort to a great deal more study of the matter (which has to be passed over here for the sake of brevity), by examining approved authors and cases from experience; on the other hand, let him carefully observe the few more important points enumerated here.

These two instructions provide advice for bishops in appointing exorcists. None of it is surprising: the priest should have the virtues of piety, prudence, integrity, constancy, and humility. Although there is no minimum age given, he should also "be of mature years."

3. Especially, he should not believe too readily that a person is possessed by an evil spirit; but he ought to ascertain the signs by which a person possessed can be distinguished from one who is suffering from some illness, especially

one of a psychological nature. Signs of possession may be the following: ability to speak with some facility in a strange tongue or to understand it when spoken by another; the faculty of divulging future and hidden events; display of powers which are beyond the subject's age and natural condition; and various other indications which, when taken together as a whole, build up the evidence.

18. The exorcist should guard against giving or recommending any medicine to the patient, but should leave this care to physicians.

We can see several important items in these sections. We see that exorcists should not be too quick to believe that a person is possessed by a demon. Although the Rite of Exorcism was published in the year 1614, shortly after the invention of the printing press, the Catholic exorcism ceremony existed in various forms for centuries before that.It may come as a shock to those who think the Middle Ages were an entirely superstitious and gullible time, but the Church never presumed that multitudes of people were demonically possessed. This is clear from the sentence that says exorcists should be careful to distinguish between demon possession and psychological disorders. Section 18 stresses that exorcists are not physicians, and should leave matters of medicine to them. Again, those who think the Church is an enemy of science would have a hard time reckoning with a medieval Church ritual that cautions exorcists about mistaking mental disorders for demon possession, and instructing those exorcists not to interfere with medicines prescribed by physicians.

A final key point in these sections is the list of three specific signs that may accompany demon possession. One is *the ability to speak or understand an unfamiliar language.* The exorcists I have read and interviewed disagree on some things, but they are all in agreement on this: the language must be a real language, one that is or was spoken by human beings. Incoherent babbling does not count as a sign of demon possession. The rite further declares that the possessed must have *some facility*, which means that it is not enough for individuals to speak or understand a few phrases of an unfamiliar language that they might have heard at some time. They must be fluent, and it must be verified that they did not know the particular language.

The second sign of demonic possession is *knowledge of future and hidden events*. As we discussed earlier, although only God knows the future in its entirety, demons have knowledge of the future that far surpasses that of human beings. Through intelligent and shrewd predictions, demons can appear to tell the future. Being spirits, they can travel anywhere in the world instantaneously; they can listen to private conversations and observe private actions; they can communicate with one another about what they see and hear; and they remember all of it. When individuals reveal knowledge of events that they could not humanly know, it may be a sign of demonic knowledge.

The third sign of demonic possession is the *display of powers that are beyond the subject's age and natural condition*. Exorcists say this is typically shown by strength beyond what a person should normally have. This sign can be tricky because other factors such as drug use can give individuals abnormal strength. Another *display of power* that fits this category is levitation, which occurs when a person's body rises from the ground. Although exorcists say this rarely occurs in cases of possession, some have seen it on at least one occasion.

Notice how these three types of activities of possessing demons seem to be deliberately mocking the power of God. For example, at Pentecost the Holy Spirit gave the apostles the miraculous ability to praise God in different languages; demons use their knowledge of all languages to blaspheme and tell lies. For his good purposes, God sometimes reveals knowledge of the future to men, such as the Old Testament prophets; demons use their intelligence to predict future events in order to frighten or astonish. Throughout history, God has granted miraculous powers to his saints in order to show his glory and accomplish his will; demons cause possessed persons to exhibit levitation, great strength, and other superhuman powers to manifest their control over them.

After enumerating the three signs, the rite states that the exorcist may take into account *various other indications which, when taken together as a whole, build up the evidence* of possession. Since these indications are not specified, exorcists have some latitude in deciding what constitutes a sign of possession.

> 6. Once in a while, after they [demons] are already recognized, they conceal themselves and leave the body practically free from every molestation, so that the victim believes himself completely delivered. Yet the exorcist may not desist until he sees the signs of deliverance.

> 9. Sometimes the devil will leave the possessed person in peace and even allow him to receive the holy Eucharist, to make it appear that he has departed. In fact, the arts and frauds of the evil one for deceiving a man are innumerable. For this reason the exorcist must be on his guard not to fall into this trap.

The possessed person is encouraged to receive Holy Communion in between each session, if possible. The ability to receive the Eucharist, however, does not always mean that the individual has been freed of the evil spirits. Demons may try various tricks to make it seem that they have been driven out, such as having possessed persons appear calm for a period of time, or having them tell the exorcist they are feeling fine. Therefore the rite warns that *the exorcist may not desist until he sees the signs of deliverance.*

> 10. Therefore, he will be mindful of the words of our Lord (Matt. 17:20), to the effect that there is a certain type of evil spirit who cannot be driven out except by prayer and fasting. Therefore, let him avail himself of these two means above all for imploring the divine assistance in expelling demons, after the example of the holy fathers; and not only himself, but let him induce others, as far as possible, to do the same.

The exorcist is reminded of Christ's words that some demons can only be driven out by prayer and fasting. Therefore, he should take time to pray and fast in preparation for the exorcism. Since exorcisms can be mentally and physically taxing, several exorcists have said that they think it best to be moderate in regard to fasting for an exorcism. For example, they may skip a meal, or consume only bread and milk on the day of the exorcism. They also have other people, such as a convent of nuns, whom they ask to pray and fast.

> 11. If it can be done conveniently, the possessed person should be led to church or to some other sacred and worthy place where the exorcism will be held, away from the crowd. But if the person is ill, or for any valid reason, the exorcism may take place in a private home.

As the rite indicates, the ideal is to perform the exorcism in a sacred place that is also private, in order to avoid attracting attention. Exorcists almost always perform the exorcism in a parish church or a small chapel, though it may be done anywhere that is convenient so long as it is private. This is to prevent the exorcism ceremony from being turned into a spectacle. I have been told by exorcists that the ceremony may be audio recorded but not video recorded. An exorcist explained to me that it is worthwhile to have audio recordings for purposes of analysis and study, but videos are more likely to be used for sensationalist purposes.

> 4. In order to understand these matters better, let him inquire of the person possessed, following one or the other act of exorcism, what the latter experienced in his body or soul while the exorcism was being performed, and to learn also what particular words in the form had a more intimidating effect upon the devil, so that hereafter these words may be employed with greater stress and frequency.

> 13. He ought to have a crucifix at hand or somewhere in sight. If relics of the saints are available, they are to be applied in a reverent way to the breast or the head of the person possessed.

> 16. If he notices that the person afflicted is experiencing a disturbance in some part of his body or an acute pain or a swelling appears in some part, he traces the sign of the cross over that place and sprinkles it with holy water, which he must have at hand for this purpose.

> 17. He will pay attention as to what words in particular cause the evil spirits to tremble, repeating them the more frequently. And when he comes to a threatening expression, he recurs to it again and again, always increasing the

punishment. If he perceives that he is making progress, let him persist for two, three, four hours, and longer if he can, until victory is attained.

Several related points can be seen in these sections. First is to note that the demons are affected by the sense perceptions of possessed individuals. The possessed may have a negative reaction to *hearing* prayers, being *touched* by holy water and relics as well as being traced with the sign of the cross, and *seeing* the crucifix. Furthermore, although section 3 of the rite clearly indicates three signs of possession, all exorcists with whom I am familiar say that a *negative reaction to the sacred* is a fourth sign of possession. Though not stated explicitly, this is implied in sections that mention a reaction to holy water, relics, the crucifix, and prayer. The 1999 rite specifically states that a negative reaction to the sacred is a sign of possession.[54]

Finally, we are given an indication as to how long the ceremony may last. A typical session may be anywhere from thirty minutes to two hours. The rite tells the exorcist not to stop at that point if a negative reaction to the sacred shows that he is making progress.

14. The exorcist must not digress into senseless prattle nor ask superfluous questions or such as are prompted by curiosity, particularly if they pertain to future and hidden matters, all of which have nothing to do with his office. Instead, he will bid the unclean spirit keep silence and answer only when asked. Neither ought he to give any credence to the devil if the latter maintains that he is the spirit of some saint or of a deceased party, or even claims to be a good angel.

15. But necessary questions are, for example: the number and name of the spirits inhabiting the patient, the

time when they entered into him, the cause thereof, and the like. As for all jesting, laughing, and nonsense on the part of the evil spirit—the exorcist should prevent it or condemn it, and he will exhort the bystanders (whose number must be very limited) to pay no attention to such goings on; neither are they to put any question to the subject. Rather they should intercede for him to God in all humility and urgency.

The Rite of Exorcism cautions the exorcist not to fall into needless discussion with demons, nor to let his curiosity lead him to ask irrelevant questions. The possessing demons may offer to give him hidden information or tell him about future events, but he is to ignore this and to command them to speak only in response to his questions. For example, one exorcist says that the demon told him: "I was standing at the cross. I was standing at Bethlehem. I was standing in Nazi Germany. I was there. What do you want to know?"[55] While avoiding superfluous questions, the exorcist may ask questions relevant to the exorcism, such as the name of the demons, their number, the cause of their possessing the victim, and the sign of their departure. The names of the demons can be particularly effective in forcing them to obey commands and answer questions. Exorcists say that the demons often lie about their names (as they do about everything else), and the way to learn whether they are lying is to command them by their names. For example, if the demon is screaming, mocking, or laughing, and does not stop despite repeated orders using the name it gave, it was probably lying.

After providing several questions that should be asked, the Rite of Exorcism adds the phrase *and the like*. As the ritual allowed for exorcists to take into account other unspecified signs, so it also gives exorcists some latitude in asking additional unspecified questions.

The rite indicates that there should be some assistants—but only a few—to *intercede* (that is, to pray) during the exorcism. They also help to restrain the possessed persons if they become physically aggressive, which happens on some occasions.

19. While performing the exorcism over a woman, he ought always to have assisting him several women of good repute, who will hold on to the person when she is harassed by the evil spirit. These assistants ought if possible to be close relatives of the subject, and for the sake of decency the exorcist will avoid saying or doing anything which might prove an occasion of evil thoughts to himself or to the others.

If the possessed person is a woman, there should be female assistants. If it is necessary for her to be restrained, women rather than men should restrain her if possible. As the American bishops state in their explanation of the new rite, "When an afflicted member of the faithful is female, there should be at least one other female present for the sake of propriety and discretion. At no time should the exorcist be alone with an afflicted member of the faithful, neither during consultation nor for the celebration of the rite."[56]

20. During the exorcism he shall preferably employ words from Holy Writ, rather than forms of his own or of someone else. He shall, moreover, command the devil to tell whether he is detained in that body by necromancy, by evil signs or amulets; and if the one possessed has taken the latter by mouth, he should be made to vomit them;

if he has them concealed on his person, he should expose them; and when discovered they must be burned. Moreover, the person should be exhorted to reveal all his temptations to the exorcist.

This section tells the exorcist that Bible passages are more powerful than prayers created by himself or someone else. It also explains another legitimate question to ask the demons, which is whether they are being kept in the body by evil signs or amulets. Examples of these are idols, symbols of false gods, and magic crystals connected with New Age practices and various cults. None of these idols, false gods, or crystals have any inherent power. However, putting faith in them is a denial of the one true God and provides an opening to the evil spirits.

21. Finally, after the possessed one has been freed, let him be admonished to guard himself carefully against falling into sin, so as to afford no opportunity to the evil spirit of returning, lest the last state of that man become worse than the former.

Serious sins weaken our relationship with God, and those who are knowingly determined to indulge in such sins are building a relationship with evil. This is especially dangerous for those who have been victims of possession: Jesus warned that if they open themselves to demons a second time, the results could be even worse (Matt. 12:43–45).

CHAPTER II: EXORCISM OF ONE POSSESSED BY A DEMON

When we think of (or see in a movie) a priest performing an exorcism, he is using this part of the rite. It contains three

exorcisms, or three times when the exorcist specifically orders the demons to depart. The exorcisms are like the opposite side of the coin of prayers: whereas prayers are spoken
to God, exorcisms are addressed to demons. The exorcisms
always invoke the power of God in ordering the demons to
leave. The ceremony also includes prayers, Bible readings,
holy water, signs of the cross, and the laying-on of hands.
The following is an outline of the Rite of Exorcism, following the numbering that appears in it.

1. The exorcist goes to confession and offers Mass before
the exorcism. The possessed person should be bound if
necessary to keep him from harming himself or the others
present. The exorcist, vested in a surplice and a violet stole,
begins by tracing the sign of the cross over the possessed
person (called an *energumen*), himself, and those assisting.
He then sprinkles all present with holy water. They kneel
and pray the litany of the saints. The exorcist prays Psalm
53, followed by a prayer asking God to cast out the devil.

2. The exorcist commands the demons to reveal their
names and the time of their departure.
    I command you, unclean spirit, whoever you are,
along with all your minions now attacking this servant of
God, by the mysteries of the Incarnation, Passion, Resur-
rection, and Ascension of our Lord Jesus Christ, by the
descent of the Holy Spirit, by the coming of our Lord
for judgment, that you tell me by some sign your name,
and the day and hour of your departure. I command you,
moreover, to obey me to the letter, I who am a minister
of God despite my unworthiness; nor shall you be em-
boldened to harm in any way this creature of God, or the
bystanders, or any of their possessions.

There follows a short prayer, which the exorcist says while laying his hand on the person's head.

3. The exorcist reads one or more of the Gospel passages that are provided, then sprinkles holy water and offers a prayer asking for the forgiveness of the person's sins.

4. The exorcist makes the sign of the cross over himself and the energumen, then places the end of his stole on the energumen's neck and his hand on his head. He says a short prayer and recites the three exorcisms, each of which concludes with a prayer. During the prayers, the exorcist repeatedly makes the sign of the cross over the person and traces the sign of the cross on the energumen's head and chest.

5. The exorcist may repeat all of the preceding until the possessed individual has been freed from the demons.

6. The exorcist may, at any time, pray the Our Father, the Hail Mary, the Creed, and any of the prayers in the following sections of the rite.

7. The exorcist prays the Canticle of the Blessed Virgin Mary (Luke 1:46–55), the Canticle of Zechariah (Luke 1:68–79), the Athanasian Creed, and the prayers following each of these. He then prays any of a number of psalms as indicated. After the demons are driven out, the priest concludes the exorcism rite with the following prayer:

Almighty God, we beg you to keep the evil spirit from further molesting this servant of yours, and to keep him far away, never to return. At your command, O Lord, may the goodness and peace of our Lord Jesus Christ, our Redeemer, take possession of this man (woman). May we no longer fear any evil since the Lord is with us; who lives and reigns with you, in the unity of the Holy Spirit, God, forever and ever. Amen.

Reading through the actual ceremony may be disappointing to those who are expecting it to be more dramatic. However, while it looks to be a rather dry process on paper, the words and actions of the possessing demons can make the exorcism "rough and tumble," as an exorcist puts it.[57] For example, one exorcist described five good-size men struggling to restrain a frail 72-year-old woman.[58] Another recalled a young man ripping the handles off the wooden chair in which he was sitting, and charging at the exorcist "like a bulldog." He stopped short when the exorcist said a quick prayer.[59]

CHAPTER III: EXORCISM OF SATAN AND THE FALLEN ANGELS

Infestation exists when demons exert their power over a particular place or thing, rather than over a human being. Chapter III of the Rite of Exorcism addresses such cases. This chapter was added in 1890 by Pope Leo XIII, and it begins with a longer version of his well-known *Prayer to St. Michael the Archangel*. It continues with another prayer, an exorcism, a final prayer, and sprinkling with holy water. Like chapter II, it indicates that a priest must be authorized by his bishop to perform the ritual. Exorcists often refer to chapter III as the *Prayers of Leo XIII*, and some use it before proceeding with an actual exorcism.

What are the specific uses for the Prayer of Leo XIII? So-called *haunted houses* may have demons attached to the house, objects within it, or the place where it is located. Whatever the case may be, this section of the rite may be prayed to drive out the demons. As we know from the Gospel story, demons can enter into animals (Matt. 8:26–33). To be precise, animals cannot be *possessed* by demons, since by definition possession refers to human beings. Demonic attacks on animals are called *infestation*, and chapter III of the Rite could be used in such cases. At least one exorcist, however, says that demon-infested animals should be killed, which he claims will prevent the demon from possessing any human beings.[60]

Bishop Thomas Paprocki of Springfield, Illinois, invoked another purpose for this section of the rite. On November 20, 2013,[61] Bishop Paprocki used the revised 2004 Rite of Exorcism, which states that this section may be used against the devil in his *opposition to and persecution of the Church*. On that date, the governor of Illinois had signed a law abolishing the definition of marriage as between one man and one woman—a definition that the Church teaches is both natural and divinely instituted, and which it upholds in the face of increasing secular opposition. Bishop Paprocki accordingly responded by praying chapter III of the rite for the protection of the Church against demonic attack.

A final purpose for chapter III is to help in discerning cases of full possession. Some exorcists use this section when they suspect, but are not certain, that individuals might be possessed. These exorcists say that chapter III may halt the demonic attack if it is lower level (i.e. oppression or obsession); and if it is a case of full possession, the prayers will provoke the demons to show themselves more clearly. Other exorcists will use chapter II—the section for cases of full possession—in order to help them discern whether or not individuals are possessed. They call this a *diagnostic exorcism*, which we will look at more closely in our chapter on the two different approaches to exorcism.

Before examining those differences, though, we will first look at the practices that most exorcists have in common.

6

The Exorcists

Exorcist is simply the title of a priest who has been appointed by his bishop to perform an exorcism. As we saw in the previous chapter, the Rite of Exorcism says that an exorcist should have the virtues of piety, prudence, integrity, constancy, and humility. The bishop may appoint a priest on a one-time basis, to perform one specific exorcism, or assign a priest to be the exorcist for the diocese. He could require the exorcist to request specific permission to perform an exorcism, or allow the exorcist to use his own judgment and perform exorcisms at his own discretion. In dioceses without an exorcist, the bishop may assign any priest to perform an exorcism, or borrow an exorcist from another diocese.

Exorcists agree that, as in most areas of life, experience is a valuable asset. The Rite of Exorcism states that exorcists should study their subject by examining cases and reading approved authors. Some priests have no particular expertise or training before they become exorcists, whereas others have assisted an exorcist periodically, or even had a sort of apprenticeship with one. Some were previously involved in healing services and deliverance, and claimed to have seen demonic attacks through this ministry. In recent years, conferences and seminars on the topics of demon possession and exorcism have been held, and priests might attend one or more of these before being assigned to perform an exorcism.

How to Contact an Exorcist

Some bishops allow their exorcists to be quite open about their role.[62] People may find an exorcist's name on a diocesan website; they may see a notice that he is going to give a talk or retreat; they may hear about him by word of mouth. If someone thinks that he or someone he knows might be possessed by demons, he should first talk to his pastor or another local priest. If he agrees that it may be a case of possession, he can contact the bishop. If the priest disagrees, one may seek a second opinion or contact the bishop's office directly.

Exorcists say that they do not have to go looking for potential cases of possession. People with worries about demonic possession seek them out regularly, whether by appointment or unannounced. Sometimes they come with referrals from other priests or through contacts at healing and deliverance services. There seems to be no shortage of persons who believe that they or someone they know is being attacked by demons.

Who Thinks They Are Possessed?

If people walked into an exorcist's office and exhibited all three signs given in the rite, it would be clear that they were possessed. However, it does not usually happen that way. They may be having *mental or emotional problems* such as feeling disconnected from reality, experiencing the sensation of an evil presence, or hearing voices telling them to commit crimes. They may have gone through a *series of crises or tragedies*; for example, they or those close to them may be suffering illness, injury, or death. Others may be coping with the break-up of close relationships, the loss of employment, or another financial calamity. Still others may have experienced *inexplicable, frightening occurrences* such as strange and unexplainable noises or voices coming from empty rooms, objects mysteriously moved or disturbed, or mechanical/ electronic devices starting or stopping of their own accord.

The exorcist, therefore, begins each case from the point of view that those who come to see him are not demonically possessed. One exorcist with whom I spoke, quoting St. Thomas Aquinas, says always to consider natural causes first. If we think about the meaning of that phrase, it is true by definition. *Natural causes* are those that follow God's usual laws of nature, so that is the first place to look for explanations. Only after those explanations are eliminated should we look to the supernatural; in this context, defined as God working outside of the laws of nature. Only after that should an exorcist consider *preternatural* explanations, such as the powers of demons.

Those who contact exorcists for help often have already decided that they are possessed. The exorcist tells them he wants to help relieve their suffering, and in order to do so, he must try to find out what is behind their problems. The cause could be spiritual, physical, mental, emotional, or a combination thereof. After the initial interview, the exorcist may accordingly consult or recommend a physician or counselor. In making this determination, the exorcist may ask questions on a range of topics:

- age, marital status, home life, family background,
- history of trauma, abuse, mental disorders, substance abuse, psychotropic medicines,
- religious affiliation, church attendance, prayer life,
- involvement with Ouija board, tarot cards, palm reading, Wicca, New Age, etc.
- books read or movies seen about the devil,
- previous experience undergoing deliverance or exorcism.

Prayer is an important part of the initial interview. Depending upon the individual exorcist, he may say prayers found in either chapter II or chapter III of the Rite of Exorcism, or he may use prayers of his own choosing.

LOGISTICS OF THE EXORCISM SESSIONS

We will use the term *session* to indicate each occasion in which the exorcist performs the exorcism rite. As we learned in the previous chapter, exorcists perform exorcisms in a sacred place, particularly a church or chapel. There should be a few other people present to pray and physically assist the exorcist in case the patient becomes physically combative. Exorcists prefer to have another priest present, but this is not always possible or practical. They may consult another priest, ideally another exorcist, before deciding to proceed with the exorcism.

Sessions typically last from thirty minutes to two hours, though the exorcist might take more time if he thinks he is making progress. Depending upon how difficult it is to coordinate the schedules of the exorcist, the assistants, and the possessed person, sessions might be performed anywhere from once a week to once a month. Some exorcists typically succeed in expelling the demons after five or ten sessions, while others report spending five or ten years. The sanctity of the exorcist, and the state of his soul, can be factors in how long the demons may resist. Therefore, as the rite indicates, the appointed priest should be noted for his maturity and moral character, and should go to confession and offer Mass before performing the exorcism.

The state of the victim's soul also influences the strength of demonic possession. A person who has long been involved in Satanism or the occult may need more sessions in order to have the demons expelled. As Jesus warned—and exorcists reiterate—such individuals must obey the exorcist's admonitions by ending all such activities and firmly resolving never to resume them.

PERSONAL PREPARATION

Exorcists stress the importance of their personal spiritual and moral lives. This includes daily prayer and receiving the sacrament of penance (confession) regularly. At Mass on the day of an exorcism, they may specifically pray for the possessed individual, or ask for the help of the saint whose feast is being celebrated that day. While none claim any moral superiority, exorcists emphasize the need for avoiding sin, especially serious sin. One exorcist described an exorcism in which another priest assisted.[63] After several sessions of making no headway, he had one session in which he suddenly made good progress against the demons. As the assisting priest was not present at that session, the exorcist decided to hold future sessions without him, and the demons were quickly expelled. It later came to light that the assisting priest had been having an affair with a woman. The exorcist said he attributed the lack of progress to the presence of the assisting priest who was engaged in habitual serious sin.

LOOKING FOR THE FOUR SIGNS OF POSSESSION

Recall the three signs of demon possession from the 1614 Rite of Exorcism: facility in a strange language, knowledge of future and hidden events, and powers beyond the natural condition. A fourth sign, as we know, is implied: a negative reaction to the sacred. Some exorcists need to see at least one of the three signs from the 1614 ritual before concluding that a person is possessed. Other exorcists say that though they might not see any of the first three signs, they become convinced of an individual's possession by the fourth sign as well as other indications. Let's examine these a little more closely.

Facility in an Unfamiliar Language

As we noted, incoherent babbling does not constitute an unfamiliar language. Exorcists are looking for a real language, whether ancient or modern. A typical example of this is when the exorcist is performing the rite in Latin, and patients who do not know that language show an understanding of it by interjecting Latin phrases or mocking the Latin prayers. One exorcist tells of a possessed young woman from Mexico who began to speak fluent Polish, recognized by a Polish-speaking priest assisting at the exorcism.[64]

As in many aspects of possession and exorcism, different exorcists report different experiences regarding this sign. One says that he never sees it, whereas another considers it the most important sign. He adds that he believes that the rite gives the three signs in order of their importance. Since facility in a strange language is listed first, it would be the most certain sign of possession, since it is listed first in the rite.[65] However, other exorcists do not attach importance to the order of the listed signs.

Knowledge of Hidden Events

This sign was dramatized in the movie *The Exorcist*, where the possessed girl reveals that the priest's mother had died, even though she had no earthly way of knowing it. Blurting out information about the private life of the exorcist—or one of those assisting him—is a typical example of hidden knowledge as a sign of possession. For example, one exorcist had spoken to a young man and concluded that he was undergoing a demonic attack. Unbeknownst to the young man, the priest consulted his bishop. The next time they met, the young man angrily said to the priest, "You told the bishop!"

Although demons cannot know our thoughts, they can observe what we do, and therefore they know our sinful actions. Interestingly, however, exorcists agree that demons do not give people knowledge of past sins that have been confessed and forgiven. Repenting of sins apparently takes away the demons' ability to use the sins as knowledge of hidden events.

Power Beyond One's Natural Condition

The most common example of this sign is physical strength beyond what the individual should normally have. We already noted an incident in which five large men could not restrain a frail seventy-two-year-old woman. Another exorcist, as he was performing the exorcism rite, would expose the body of Christ in a monstrance. He kept this at a safe distance from the possessed individual so that the host contained in the monstrance would not be desecrated or damaged. On one occasion, a possessed woman spat at the monstrance, hitting it from farther away than it seemed humanly possible to do. Despite having her eyes shut tightly, and despite one of the assistants repeatedly moving the monstrance, she continued to hit the monstrance accurately with her spittle.[66]

Another occurrence that might fit this category is an individual's eyes rolling backward or forward. This manifestation raises a thorny problem, since anyone can roll his eyes such that they appear *mostly* white—the pupil and iris barely visible. This rolling of eyes frequently happens when people faint or have seizures. But if someone's eyes rolled and appeared *completely* white, with no pupil or iris showing at all, this might be an occurrence outside of nature.

In *The Exorcist,* there was another dramatic scene in which the victim levitated. In real-life cases of possession, this is rare, but it does occasionally happen. On the other hand, in regard to that movie's best-known scene, I know of no exorcist who has seen a possessed person's head turn around a complete 360 degrees!

A Fourth Sign: Negative Reaction to the Sacred

The 1614 rite implies, and the 1999 rite explicitly states, that there is a fourth sign: negative reaction to the sacred. *Blasphemy* may be one such reaction. Blasphemy occurs when someone uses words or actions to show hate or contempt against God, his angels or saints, or sacred objects such as a crucifix. Other negative reactions to the sacred that exorcists have described include:

- laughing, snorting, howling,
- showing annoyance, repugnance, horror,
- spitting, vomiting, convulsing,
- shouting, screaming, threatening,
- physical aggression, and violence.

Some exorcists consider negative reactions to the sacred to be the most common sign of demonic possession. Others say that these reactions alone are not strong indicators, since they may occur among those who are suffering from lesser demonic attacks (obsession or oppression). Such reactions are also seen in individuals who mistakenly believe themselves to be possessed. Those who are mentally or emotionally disturbed may react negatively to religious themes because of their disorders. Whether such themes involve persons (such as the exorcist in his priestly garb), prayers, or objects such as holy water or a crucifix, a mentally disturbed person who is obsessed with such matters may have strong adverse reactions to them.

Exorcists are aware that this can be problematic, so they try to take precautions. They might try to elicit a negative reaction to ordinary water from a holy water bottle, which would suggest a mental problem rather than demonic possession. The opposite method may also be attempted: one exorcist, who suspected a woman was possessed, gave her a glass of holy water to drink without identifying it as such. She took one drink and spat it across the table. The exorcist considered this a sign that she was possessed.[67]

Periods of Crisis

Individuals who are possessed do not show these and other potential signs twenty-four hours a day, seven days a week. Signs may manifest in reaction to the sacred, but they also may occur at random. Exorcists call these times *periods of crisis*, which may last from a few minutes to many hours. As a rule, an exorcist does not conclude that a person is possessed based on a second-hand report of such crises; he must observe the signs himself. As we noted, part of the exorcist's initial interview consists of praying for the troubled individuals. If the victim is suffering from a lower level demonic attack, these prayers can ward off the demons and help the victim feel more peaceful. Similarly, in my work with those suffering from mental and emotional disorders, I have found that prayer and holy water can provide at least a brief period of calm. With full demonic possession, though, the result is usually the opposite: a prayer session can trigger a full-blown period of crisis in which the signs of possession appear.

Frightening Occurrences During the Ceremony

During an exorcism, in addition to the signs of possession exhibited by an energumen, often there are unnatural occurrences that are not directly linked to his body. Exorcists and those assisting them report physical and sensory manifestations including detached voices, foul smells, moving objects, electronic devices turning on and off, and a drastic drop in temperature. These sound frightening, like something from a horror movie or a haunted house come to life. Exorcists agree that these goings-on alarm them at first, but as they perform more exorcisms, it becomes easier to ignore them. Most exorcists say that there is no need to be afraid during an exorcism, and those present should not give in to fear. One exorcist calls these manifestations "cheap parlor tricks" while another says they're just "noise [and] distraction."[68]

Another exorcist did relate to me a dangerous encounter he had in dealing with a possessed individual. She was brought to him by her (male) friend, and the three of them went to the chapel. When they reached the doors, she was inexplicably unable to enter under her own power: it took both men to help her into the chapel. As they were praying, she pulled a knife she had kept hidden in her sweater and threw it across the chapel, narrowly missing him.

In the possession case that was the inspiration for the movie *The Exorcist*, the victim was a fourteen-year-old boy in Washington, D.C. At one point, the boy was lying in bed as the exorcist was performing the ritual. When he finished the last line of the Lord's Prayer—*deliver us from evil*—the boy slashed the full length of the exorcist's arm with a spring he had some-how worked loose from the bed. The gash required more than one hundred stitches. The exorcist did not complete the cer-emony, and a different priest was appointed for the case.[69]

Devil Commentary

Although not as dramatic as physical manifestations, com-ments made by the demons can be quite disconcerting. For example, one priest who was assisting at an exorcism was kneeling off to the side and silently praying a litany, repeat-edly asking the saints to come to the possessed woman's aid. At one point the possessed woman turned toward him and said, "No one is coming to her assistance."[70] On another occasion the same priest was assisting when the exorcist yawned noticeably. The demon laughed and said, "You're going to get tired before we do."[71]

One exorcist was saying the prayers of the ceremony for some length of time when, in his own voice, the possessed man calmly said, "Thank you for what you've done today. I feel so much better." However, when the exorcist ignored the comment and continued the prayers, the man's voice changed and the demon shouted, "I said I was okay!"[72]

The Possessing Demons

Rarely—if ever—are victims possessed by one individual demon alone, and so the 1614 rite stresses the necessity of asking about the *number* of possessing demons. Exorcists are in agreement that possession typically involves multiple demons, with one being the leader and the most difficult to expel. The switch from one demon to another may be indicated by changes in the person's personality, voice, and facial expression. (Exorcists must be certain that they are not mistaking multiple demons with manifestations of dissociative identity disorder. With experience, they learn that the shift from one demon to another in a possessed person is more subtle than the personality changes in persons with DID.) Aside from the discernment of the exorcist, the possessed individuals may report the sensation of multiple demonic presences, especially as the demons are being expelled. The number of demons typically ranges from few to a few dozen. One exorcist describes an occasion in which he believed a woman was possessed by hundreds of demons.

The Rite of Exorcism also instructs exorcists to ask the demons to reveal their names. On one occasion, Jesus asked the name of the demons whom he was driving out of a man. They responded, "My name is Legion; for we are many" (Mark 5:9). On the other occasions when Jesus expelled demons, though, the Gospels do not report him asking for their names. Perhaps that is why exorcists vary in the emphasis they place on the importance of learning the names of the demons. However, they agree that learning the demons' names can be a means of gaining power over them.

Consequently, demons resist revealing their names, and, as one exorcist expressed it, they must "beat it out of them." The Rite of Exorcism indicates that the exorcist may repeat the prayers and commands, sprinkle holy water, show the crucifix, trace the sign of the cross, and touch the victim with relics of saints. Certain factors can make it more difficult to force demons to reveal their names. These are the same factors that affect the difficulty of expelling the demons, such as the sanctity and state of soul of the exorcist, and the depth of the victim's entanglements with evil. Since God and the Church are stronger, the demons will eventually be forced either to depart or tell their names.

When the demons do finally provide names, the exorcist may test them to see whether they have lied. For example, the exorcist may use a demon's name in commanding it to say a certain phrase, such as *Hail Mary*. If his command is not obeyed, the demon has probably lied, and the exorcist must continue to demand that it give its true name. If it has been laughing, mocking, or speaking about things when not asked, the exorcist may use its name in ordering it to be silent. Again, if it does not obey, he presumes the demon has not revealed its true name.

THE BLESSED VIRGIN MARY

The Rite of Exorcism encourages repeated praying of the Hail Mary. One exorcist notes "how much Mary is hated by the evil one," theorizing that this is because they could not accept that God would become a human being, and that he did so in Mary's womb. Another adds:

> My whole devotion and understanding of Our Lady has changed night and day . . . in the role she plays, how much she is hated by the evil one—absolute hatred of the Mother of God, and the power she wields in all of this.[73]

Another exorcist explains how he asks for her help when he is not making progress in the exorcism:

> Sometimes you get your back to the wall. Just stop and invite the Blessed Virgin Mary in to stomp on the head of this serpent, and say the Hail Mary. Ask her to come and take care of this. So I use that quite a bit.[74]

This exorcist was referring to a passage from the book of Genesis, in which God tells the serpent, Satan, that a descendant of Adam and Eve will crush his head. The war between the Blessed Virgin and the devil is mentioned again in the book of Revelation, where Mary appears as "a woman clothed with the sun, with the moon under her feet, and on her head a crown of twelve stars" (12:1). Satan is waiting to destroy her and her child, but is defeated after her child, Jesus, is taken up to God's throne and Mary is given a special place of protection.

Are the Demons Gone?

How does an exorcist know when all of the demons have been driven out once and for all? The instructions of the Rite state:

> 6. Once in a while, after they are already recognized, they conceal themselves and leave the body practically free from every molestation, so that the victim believes himself completely delivered. Yet the exorcist may not desist until he sees the signs of deliverance.

Exorcists say that one obvious indication that the demons are gone is that the four signs have stopped manifesting for an extended period. They also look for an abiding sense of peace to come over the energumen. Demons may shriek when they are driven out, as seen in the Gospels (Luke 4:33–41) and reported by exorcists. The possessed individuals themselves may have a sense of their departure. Sometimes there is a noticeable peculiar exhaling from the nose and/or mouth that accompanies the exodus of the demons.

The exorcist may also order the demons to give a specific sign when they are driven out. One exorcist describes such a scene:

[During] one exorcism I was involved in, the command was given as a sign of departure to say, "Hail Mary, full of grace." Then the demon responded by saying, "Grace thou full." [The demon] scrambled the words, never said the name of the Blessed Mother, but scrambled the words around and then laughed. And then [the exorcist gave] the command, given in the name of Christ, to say the words in order; the demon was commanded to say them. The demon then said, "Hail Mary, full of grace," and then shrieked. Then the person—just like that—said, "How are you doing, Father?"[75]

AFTER THE EXORCISM

An exorcist typically instructs possessed individuals to follow a strong daily prayer routine between sessions. When the demons are finally expelled and the sessions have ended, he admonishes them to continue this. The exorcist also encourages a spiritual discipline that includes a number of aspects.

First, the individuals should work on the areas that opened the door to the demonic possession in the first place. Occult activities such as Satanism, witchcraft, and use of the Ouija board must be abandoned, as should consultations with palm readers, psychics, and horoscopes. They should take steps to overcome habits of serious sin, such as drug and alcohol abuse, sexual promiscuity, and pornography.

These sinful habits should be replaced with good spiritual habits. Catholics should establish a daily prayer life including such things as Scripture reading, the rosary, and use of holy water. They should attend Mass every week and go to confession regularly. Similarly, non-Catholics should pursue a daily prayer life and weekly church attendance.

Furthermore, the freed individuals should try to restore good relationships they may have abandoned. One exorcist gives the example of Jesus driving the devils from the Gerasene demoniac. When this possessed man was freed, he wanted to follow Jesus, but Jesus told him: "Go home to your family and make it clear to them how much the Lord in his mercy has done for you" (Mark 5:1–20). Accordingly, this exorcist tells the freed individuals how important it is for them to reconnect with their family and faith community.[76]

After successful exorcisms, the exorcist encourages the freed individuals to contact him for regular follow-up conversations for about a year. If he believes they are also suffering from a mental or emotional disorder, he will encourage them to continue seeing a counselor or psychologist. When the exorcist no longer hears from them, he presumes these individuals are doing well. Jesus indicated that it is possible for a freed person to be possessed again by even worse demons than the first (Matt. 12:43–45), and exorcists warn about this possibility. However, they say that they rarely see this happen, perhaps because individuals who have experienced and been delivered from demonic possession are eager to do anything that will stop it from happening again.

~

In some important respects, all exorcists follow the same process. They are appointed by their bishop. They ask the same basic questions about a person's physical, mental, spiritual, and family history. If they think the root of the problem is not spiritual, they recommend appropriate medical or psychological treatment. They maintain a strong prayer life for themselves, and pray for those in their care. They may consult other exorcists and have other priests assist in sessions. They look for similar signs of possession and of the departure of demons.

The rite's instructions, however, leave some room for the exorcist's private judgment. We have seen some examples of this already, in the way exorcists assign varying degrees of importance to different signs of possession. The rite also gives leeway to exorcists in discerning other indications of possession. These and other areas where exorcists may use their own judgment within the rite have given rise to two distinct approaches taken by exorcists today, which we will examine in the next chapter.

7

Two Approaches to Exorcism

Even though Catholic exorcists follow the same ritual, they don't follow it in exactly the same way. In my inquiry into the exorcism process, I found that exorcists tend to take one of two basic approaches, which I will call the *narrow approach* and the *wide approach*.[77]

Several disclaimers are needed before we look at these terms. First, I want to emphasize that these are not official Church methods or teachings; neither are these approaches recognized by exorcists themselves. Rather, they are differences I have noticed as an outsider—a priest who is not an exorcist—researching their work. Second, it is important to note that although a particular exorcist will largely follow one approach, commonly he will employ some aspects of the other as well. Finally, no matter which approach exorcists use, they all show a keen awareness that it is not just the approach they use, but also the state of their own souls that has an effect on their power to drive out demons.

What do I mean by the terms narrow and wide? In the narrow approach, exorcists take little latitude within the rite, even where they are allowed to do so. In the wide approach, exorcists interpret the directives of the rite more broadly. In the narrow approach, exorcists perform exorcisms only if individuals exhibit a few specifically defined criteria, whereas wide approach exorcists perform exorcisms based on a larger range of criteria. The narrow approach exorcist believes that he need only follow the ritual and the demons will be expelled. In the wide approach, exorcists add a number of other questions, tests, and categorizations that they believe are important—and possibly necessary—to perform a successful exorcism.

SIGNS OF POSSESSION

In the narrow approach, the exorcist determines whether individuals are possessed by looking for the three signs listed in the exorcism rite: facility in an unknown language, knowledge of hidden events, and powers beyond the natural condition. Seeing just one sign is probably not going to convince him, because there is room for error. For example, inordinate strength may be a sign of demonic possession, but it may also be the result of a drug overdose or a psychotic episode. The exorcist may consider other behaviors to be indicative of lower level demonic attacks (oppression, obsession, infestation), but he wants to see at least one more of the three signs before concluding it is a case of full demonic possession. He does not perform the exorcism unless and until he believes an individual is possessed. This approach corresponds with the 1999 Rite of Exorcism, which instructs the priest to have "moral certitude" that individuals are possessed before performing an exorcism. As one exorcist says, "The Church doesn't want to be too stingy with the Rite of Exorcism, but it also doesn't want a sideshow mentality."[78]

An exorcist who follows the wide approach also looks for the three signs of possession, but he believes that some of these signs might appear only after he has begun the exorcism. Exorcists call this method a *diagnostic exorcism:* the rite itself is used to determine whether or not an individual is possessed. One exorcist says:

It is my significant experience, and that of all the other

exorcists whom I questioned, that these signs always sur-
faced during an exorcism, never before. It would be quite
unrealistic to expect the manifestation of those signs before proceeding with the exorcism."[79]

The fourth sign—negative reaction to the sacred—is considered highly significant in the wide approach, and may even
be taken as the determinant. The exorcist also takes into account a host of other sense perceptions and behaviors. Indeed,
for exorcists who follow the wide approach, the list of signs of
demonic possession can be quite extensive, including:

PHYSICAL MANIFESTATIONS

- headaches,
- unexplained pains in the stomach, kidneys, and ovaries,
- lack of effectiveness of medicines,
- eyes rolling backward so that the pupils are barely visible,
- strange gesticulations of the hands, facial twitching, total
  loss of energy,
- convulsions, contortions, falling to the ground, rigidity.

MENTAL HEALTH PROBLEMS

- violent behavior, including kicking, biting, and scratch-
  ing,
- suicidal tendencies,
- temptations to commit murder and other crimes.

DETERIORATION IN LIFE SITUATIONS

- breakdown of marriage, family, and other personal relationships,

- sudden inability to study or learn,
- financial, employment, and business problems.

Changes in Personality

- impulsive, offensive comments,
- withdrawal, isolation, refusal to converse, or difficulty in expressing oneself,
- fascination with evil and the occult.

Effects on Consciousness and the Senses

- horrible nightmares and vivid waking terrors,
- a stupor or trance-like state; disconnection from reality,
- feeling of an evil presence, unseen person, or vaguely visible shadow,
- audible hallucinations, mental chatter and noise, voices that threaten punishment or blaspheme God.

External Phenomena

- hysteria of individuals near the possessed person,
- unexplainable lights,
- mechanical failures,
- objects materializing and dematerializing.

The Screening Process

The screening process begins with a challenge: people who approach an exorcist for help are presuming they are possessed by demons, whereas the exorcist begins by presuming they are not. This is true of exorcists in general, regardless of which approach they use. As one exorcist explained, "I will tell people, 'You need the help you truly need, perhaps not what you think you need. So let's determine whether this is really of a mental nature or a spiritual nature.'"[80] Another agrees: "I tend to be extremely cautious, presuming always that there is some kind of psychological anomaly or some kind of mental health issue. That's my point of departure . . . the exorcist is trained as a skeptic."[81] The American bishops' recent explanation of exorcism supports this approach: "Only after a thorough examination including medical, psychological, and psychiatric testing might the person be referred to the exorcist for a final determination regarding demonic possession."[82]

The narrow approach exorcist typically has several sessions with the individuals. These may include the prayers of Leo XIII, other prayers and Bible readings, holy water, and other sacramentals. The exorcist will also outline a careful prayer life for the individuals to follow before the next session. This screening process serves a twofold purpose. First, if the problem turns out to be a lower level demonic attack, these prayer sessions may be enough to drive off the evil spirits. Second, if a person is possessed, the prayers may trigger the demons to react and manifest the signs from the exorcism rite. If some of these signs manifest during the initial interview, the exorcist may proceed immediately with the exorcism, provided he has a proper place and people to assist him. The narrow approach also emphasizes the importance of mental health assessment and treatment, and will refer to psychological reports and therapist input to help confirm judgments regarding possession.

An exorcist using the wide approach also begins with prayers, Bible readings, holy water, and other sacramentals. However, he does not need to see the signs from the rite. If the individuals react by showing some of the many signs that are not in the rite, the exorcist proceeds with the exorcism. If it turns out the individuals are fully possessed, they may begin to manifest the signs from the rite; if they are victims of a lower level demonic attack, the rite helps to drive off the demons. If it turns out there is no demonic presence, the wide-approach exorcist believes there is no harm done in having performed the rite. Exorcists using the wide approach may also consult mental health professionals, but do not consider it to be as important as narrow approach exorcists do.

Types of Demons

Jesus and the apostles drove out demons on many occasions, but only a few times in Scripture is the *type* of demon mentioned—with the phrases *dumb and deaf spirit, spirit of infirmity,* and *spirit of divination* indicating the effect that each demon had on its victim (Mark 9:16–27; Luke 13:10–16; Acts 16:16–18). Other than those exceptions, the New Testament does not mention different types of demons. Likewise, the Rite of Exorcism does not mention different types of demons, nor does it offer different methods for expelling them. Therefore, for exorcists who follow the narrow approach, it does not matter whether or not there are different types, since they perform the rite in essentially the same way each time.

Exorcists who follow the wide approach, however, emphasize the importance of knowing what kinds of demons are possessing the individuals, because they may tailor the way they conduct the exorcism accordingly. One well-known exorcist talks about *abditi* or *hidden* demons, which do not immediately manifest in any way. This exorcist says that the only initial indication of their presence is that the possessed person "notices a change in his life and feels strange things that make him suspect there is an external force that has entered him."[83] The exorcist may pray for hours and still see no signs of possession. Eventually, though, if the energumen keeps a consistent prayer life and also meets with the exorcist regularly for prayer session, the hidden demons will be forced to reveal their presence through the usual signs.

As a priest and counselor who visits mentally disturbed patients on a daily basis, I frequently meet individuals who suspect that an external force has entered them. My approach is to say a prayer and sprinkle them with holy water, and encourage them to pray daily to protect themselves from demons. I also tell them that demon possession is extremely rare, and that unless they demonstrate unnatural powers, they are not possessed. I do not want to reinforce the idea of demonic possession in the mind of a mentally disturbed person who is already fixated on the devil.

The same exorcist mentioned above also states that there are *aperti* and *clausi*, or *open* and *closed* demons. This refers to whether the demon keeps the victim's eyes open or closed during the exorcism. The *aperti*, he says, "[Give] looks of anger and rage [and] are loquacious and violent, and the possessed person often needs to be held down during the exorcism."[84] As a result, if the exorcist finds he is dealing with *aperti*, he must have several physically strong assistants to restrain the possessed person during the exorcism. By contrast, the *clausi* cause the energumen to enter a trance during the exorcism, and they may not speak at all. If faced with *clausi,* he must not be too quick to believe the exorcism has succeeded, since the demon may simply be remaining quiet.

Another exorcist says there are four types of demons that are related to the means by which they possess individuals.[85] *Occult demons* enter as a result of occult activity; *demons of sin* through long habits of sin; *trauma demons* through trauma and abuse; and *generational spirits* that are attached to whole families, often for several generations or more. This exorcist prescribes slightly different approaches for each type. He says the occult demons are the most difficult to exorcise, and require renunciation of the activity. Those possessed by demons of sin must renounce the particular type of sin by name. To drive out trauma demons, the victim must forgive those who perpetrated the trauma, and the exorcist must say prayers for inner healing. When confronting generational spirits, the exorcist must pray for the victim's family tree.

Exorcists following the narrow approach likewise encourage possessed individuals to stop occult practices, forgive those who have hurt them, and confess their sins. These exorcists, however, do not find it necessary to tailor specific prayers to certain types of demons; neither does the Rite of Exorcism make mention of them. Moreover, the jargon of *renouncing* particular sins (rather than expressing contrition for them and having a firm purpose of amendment) seems more Pentecostal than Catholic. Perhaps it's no coincidence that this exorcist credits this methodology to a former priest who left the Church and is now involved in a worldwide deliverance ministry.[86]

CURSED OBJECTS

Another difference in approach involves the treatment of cursed objects, which may be called amulets, charms, or idols. The Rite of Exorcism contains the following instruction:

> He shall, moreover, command the devil to tell whether he is detained in that body by necromancy, by evil signs or amulets; and if the one possessed has taken the latter by mouth, he should be made to vomit them; if he has them concealed on his person, he should expose them; and when discovered they must be burned.

If the victims admit to having more such objects elsewhere, the narrow approach exorcist tells them to either burn the objects or bring them back for him to burn. If the objects are made of nonflammable material such as metal or ceramic, the exorcist may bend, break, or otherwise deface them; he may sprinkle them with holy water; or he may dispose of them by burying them or throwing them into a body of water.

In the wide approach, the process may be more elaborate. One exorcist recommends that amulets be sprinkled with holy water, then burned while prayers are said; afterward, the ashes must be thrown into running water. He cautions that failure to follow these steps can cause serious health problems.[87] Another warns that the exorcist should try not to touch such objects, but if he must do so, he should then wash his hands with holy water.[88] In contrast, an exorcist who follows the narrow approach told me, "The key is not to become fixated on how to treat them, or to give them more power than they actually possess."

TALKING TO DEMONS

Exorcists also differ in their approach to addressing or conversing with possessing demons. The rite includes the following caution:

> [The] exorcist must not digress into senseless prattle nor ask superfluous questions or such as are prompted by curiosity . . . But necessary questions are, for example: the number and name of the spirits inhabiting the patient, the time when they entered into him, the cause thereof, and the like.

In the narrow approach, the exorcists ask only these questions. One describes the process as follows: "The exorcist continues to harp away at, 'What's your name? How did you enter? When are you going to leave?' Those are the three questions, over and over again."[89] These exorcists are also restrained in speaking to demons, saying little other than the prayers and exorcisms as directed in the exorcism rite. As one exorcist explains, "Do not get in a conversation with the demon."[90]

In the wide approach, in addition to what is found in the rite, the exorcist may engage the demons with a multitude of questions, discussions, and tests. These involve topics such as the sin committed by the demons, the origin of hell, and the relationships that exist among the souls in hell. One exorcist posed a philosophical challenge to the demon:

Explain to me the meaning of reclaiming your freedom before God when you are nothing if you are separated from him, just as I am nothing. It is as though, in the number ten, the zero wanted to be separated from the number one. What would it become? What would it accomplish? I command you, in the name of God, tell me what you achieved that is positive? Come on, speak![91]

Another exorcist tells of casually threatening demons with the invocation of two recently canonized saints, Pope St. John Paul II and St. Pio of Pietrelcina: "Well, I will just have to call on the Polish Pope to deal with you . . . Should I call my priest friend with the stigmata to get you to leave?"[92]

Spiritual Gifts

The Rite of Exorcism says nothing about *spiritual gifts*— receiving direct messages or knowledge from God—so the narrow approach exorcists do not attach much importance to them. Those who follow the wide approach, on the other hand, may greatly value—even depend on—spiritual gifts in carrying out exorcisms. For example, in one case an exorcist received word from another priest that a particular case was useless and that he should give up on it. Since the exorcist believed the priest possessed spiritual gifts, he stopped the exorcism.[93] On another occasion, an exorcist thought a woman was possessed, but when a priest with alleged spiritual gifts said she was not, the exorcist decided not to perform an exorcism.[94] Wide approach exorcists may also depend on such spiritual gifts to find out how many demons are possessing an individual, and to identify each demon as it departs.[95]

Did It Work?

Exorcists who follow the narrow approach report a 100 percent success rate under one condition: possessed individuals must cooperate in the process. Cooperation consists of ending any Satanic or occult practices in which they have been engaged, repenting of patterns of serious sin, and following the spiritual discipline given to them by the exorcist. If, as is typical, the sessions are conducted every week or two, it may take from three to six months to successfully complete the exorcism. It would be rare to drive out all of the demons in the first session, and it would be similarly rare to require more than a dozen sessions.

In the wide approach, there are occasions when the exorcist cannot successfully drive out the demons, even if the possessed person cooperates.[96] The problem could be with the exorcist: "[He] could be doing things that are ineffective with a particular demon."[97] However, there could be an outside force involved: "There may also be some strong occult force that gives the demon or the possession extra power."[98] Exorcists who follow the wide approach often report many more sessions and much more time to expel all of the demons than narrow approach exorcists. A few months to complete an exorcism is considered a short process, and in more difficult cases, the exorcist may conduct weekly sessions for many years.[99] Even after performing exorcisms regularly for more than fifteen years, these exorcists who follow the wide approach may be unable to free victims from the possessing demons.[100]

WHERE DO THE DEMONS GO?

The Rite of Exorcism makes no comment as to where demons go when they are expelled; the exorcist simply states: "I cast you out, unclean spirit . . . Begone and stay far from this creature of God." Since exorcists who follow the narrow approach adhere strictly to the words of the rite, they do not believe there is a need to address this.

Among exorcists who use the wide approach, however, the destination of demons after they are expelled is a topic of interest. One says, "An exorcist should command the demons to go to the foot of the cross or to go directly to Jesus. Some think that demons should be sent back to hell, but the priest does not have this authority!"[101]

The same exorcist explains what he means by the phrase *the foot of the cross*: "[It] is the *spiritual* place of our redemption which stands outside of time and space. . . . it is the ultimate Tribunal where Christ judges all demons because it was the place where Satan himself was judged."[102] He adds that demons must be ordered to go there *directly*: without this specific instruction, they might stop and harass other people on their way.[103] Such ideas are legitimate as theological opinion, but are not mentioned in the Bible, the Rite of Exorcism, or the *Catechism*.

Another exorcist writes, "In the majority of cases, when they leave a soul they are destined to go to hell; at times they are freed in the desert. . . . I always force them to go at the foot of the cross, to receive their sentence from Jesus Christ, who is the sole judge."[104] This exorcist refers to the Old Testament book of Tobit, but there is a contrast between his idea that demons are sometimes *freed* in the desert, and the demon Asmodeus being *bound* there by the archangel Raphael.

INCREDIBLE STORIES

Any exorcist who has observed the three (or four) signs of demonic possession has observed something extraordinary; and the narrow approach exorcists I have interviewed do not generally have much more to say. Exorcists who adhere to the wide approach, on the other hand, are more likely to report stories with sometimes-lurid details that go beyond these signs.

The Back-and-Forth Demon

In one story, an exorcist reports sending a demon back and forth between two young girls:[105]

Once, while exorcising a young girl, [the exorcist] asked the demon his name. "Zebulun," he answered. When the exorcism was over, the priest sent the girl to pray in front of the tabernacle. When the next girl came to be exorcised, [he] asked this demon too for his name. The answer was the same: "Zebulun." The priest asked, "Are you the same demon who possessed the other girl? I command you, in the name of God, to go back to the girl you just left." The new girl uttered a sort of a howl and then became quiet and appeared calm. In the meantime, the people who were in the room heard the girl who was praying at the tabernacle take up the same howl. Then [he] ordered, "Come here again." Immediately, the new girl began the same howling, and the other girl began to pray. In these cases, possession is obvious.

Devil Lights

Another exorcist describes in his book the following experience:

> I remember the case of a man who was certain he had seen lights enter his house through the window. I examined him but did not see any signs of possession. The problem was that the entire family had seen the phenomenon and confirmed his story. I recommended he do the following: take the medication prescribed by his psychiatrist and follow all his recommendations [and] go to Mass and pray the Rosary. If it was a psychiatric problem, he was doing well seeking medical treatment and should see some improvement; if the problem was demonic in nature, though, God would hear his prayers. Of course he could return to see me in a month or two . . . After some time, the man did return to see me. It became clear that this was a case of possession.[106]

Cats, Snakes, and Birds

An exorcist describes the case of a lower level demonic attack in which he did not perform the exorcism ritual but instead performed his own method of deliverance. He believed that the woman was being attacked by demons with names and corresponding attributes: "Black Cats (this one hissed and put up claws), Innocence (this one spoke with a deceptively sweet, innocent voice), Pride (this one sat upright as if indignant and said, 'I don't have to leave')."[107]

On another occasion, this exorcist faced two demons with animal characteristics:

> It was apparent from the beginning that there was some kind of serpent demon, because, when I first placed the crucifix on her head, Angie slid out of the chair and on to the floor like a snake . . . Then we dealt with another demon that described itself as a "black bird." When this demon was present, her face took on a bird-like appearance: the nose subtly narrowed like a beak, the eyes slanted and the mouth tightened and protruded somewhat.[108]

Hundreds and Thousands of Demons

One exorcist recounts an experience with "a middle-aged woman [who] needed to be delivered from a host of lesser-strength demons which had literally infested her body."[109] The Rite of Exorcism was not needed because they were weaker demons. The exorcist proceeded to expel the demons with his own system of deliverance. In the process, he says, he and an assistant counted several hundred distinct demons that exited the possessed woman's body. Another exorcist claims to have expelled no fewer than 160,000 demons in the course of many exorcisms.[110]

Cursed Objects in Hidden Places

One exorcist says that he has found many cursed objects, such as chunks of wood or iron string and wool braided by superhuman strength, and animals, especially mice, in the mattresses and pillows of possessed people. Sometimes, he says, these objects don't materialize until he sprinkles holy water or touches the area with a crucifix. He says that cursed objects must be burned or thrown into running water, such as a river or sewer, and warns that if they are thrown into a toilet or sink, every drain may become plugged and the house may be flooded.[111]

Another exorcist says he learned from a possessing demon that the victim had hidden a cursed object in a buried box. He found the box and burned everything in it, but in the process the exorcist touched the objects and did not immediately wash his hands with holy water. As a result, he suffered from a stomach ache that lasted ten years.[112]

~

In this chapter we have seen that there are two significantly different methods by which Catholic exorcists perform exorcisms. The difference arises from the latitude that the Rite of Exorcism gives exorcists in considering signs not listed therein, and in the questions and comments directed toward the demons. As a priest and as a mental health professional, I much prefer the narrow approach; I see multiple theological and practical problems with the wide approach.

One such problem is the practice of diagnostic exorcism, in which the exorcist performs the ritual as a means of discerning whether a person is possessed. In individuals who mistakenly believe themselves to be possessed, addressing the non-existent demons can reinforce their false beliefs and thereby exacerbate their mental health problems. Similarly, I think it is improper for exorcists to see specific physical, mental, relational, and personality problems as the result of demonic attacks. Although I have no doubt that demons can and do cause such problems, it is impossible to know the extent to which demons may be responsible for any particular occurrence. A thorough mental health assessment can help discern between spiritual and mental problems, and the narrow approach is superior in emphasizing such screening over the judgments of those with self-proclaimed spiritual gifts.

A second flaw in the wide approach is its presumptive familiarity with the spirit world. For example, exorcists following this approach claim knowledge of different types of demons and of corresponding methods for dealing with them. But none of this is doctrinal, and wide approach exorcists themselves are not in agreement. The conversational tone and extensive questioning of demons is another instance of the wide approach exorcists' apparent intimacy with the demons. These practices can make exorcism appear to be melodramatic and even foolish. The narrow approach expels demons more quickly, and with less concern about the intricacies of the demonic.

Finally, one of the more striking findings of my research is the difference in tone between the narrow approach exorcists I interviewed and the wide approach exorcists who have written books on the subject. These books include first-hand stories of incredible and frightening manifestations, such as a demon jumping from one person to another, objects materializing from nowhere, and individuals infested by literally hundreds of demons. Exorcists following the narrow approach acknowledge that one individual may be possessed by numerous demons, that demons may give possessed people powers beyond their natural capacity, and that demons can cause frightening disturbances. These exorcists, however, downplay such demonic activity, describing it in terms such as *distractions* and *noise*. I wholeheartedly agree with this approach: emphasizing the more alarming goings-on plays into the demons' attempt to instill fear, and gives the appearance of sensationalism.

There is a closely related topic in which the Church needs to guard against histrionics, needless complexity, and false claims of knowledge of demons and their activity: namely, the concept and practice of *deliverance*, which we will consider in the following chapter.

8

"Deliverance" Drama

The *Catechism of the Catholic Church* gives three meanings for the word *exorcism*: the act of driving out demons; the Rite of Exorcism; and the specific prayers in the rites of baptism and exorcism in which demons are commanded to depart. The Code of Canon Law, which also briefly addresses exorcism, adds that a priest can only perform exorcisms with his bishop's approval, and that bishops should appoint priests who possess the virtues of piety, knowledge, prudence, and integrity of life. The 1999 rite includes an appendix of prayers that may be said on occasions when lower level demonic attacks (oppression and obsession) are suspected. They are called *Supplications which May be Used by the Faithful Privately in Their Struggle against the Powers of Darkness*, and they may be said by any priest or layman; a bishop's permission is not necessary.[113]

But what, if anything, does the Church have to say about *deliverance*? Catholics sometimes use that word in reference to driving out demons. Every time we pray the Our Father, we conclude by asking God to *deliver us from evil*. There is no Catholic doctrine on deliverance, no official explanation of what it is or how it is to be done, no Church ceremony or liturgy, and no one authorized or appointed to perform deliverance. And yet, the idea and practice of deliverance is a vital part of the spiritual life for a small percentage of Catholics who think of it as a kind of liturgical rite.

I will refer to such Catholics as *deliverance enthusiasts*, and their leaders I will call *deliverance professionals*. These are not intended to be derogatory terms. The first accurately de-scribes those who are enthusiastic about the topic of deliver-ance from demons. The second identifies those who speak at conferences on deliverance, write books on the topic, or claim to perform deliverances. They may prefer the term deliverance *minister*, but I will not use that title because it gives the false impression that they are functioning in some official Church role.

Who Are the Deliverance Professionals?

There is a branch of Protestantism called Pentecostalism, the followers of which believe that they commonly receive supernatural gifts from God. These include miraculous healing powers, knowledge of other people's thoughts and personal history, and messages regarding difficult decisions. Another important belief of the followers of this spirituality is that they can possess an awareness of the activity of de-mons, and the power to expel them.

In the late 1960s, some Catholics began bringing Pen-tecostal spirituality into the Church. This started with stu-dents and instructors at Duquesne University who had been reading books written by Pentecostals, attending their prayer services, and inviting them to instruct Catholics in their spirituality.[114] In addition to imitating the alleged extraordi-nary gifts of the Holy Spirit they learned of, some Catholics wished to drive out demons in the same dramatic fashion as their Pentecostal counterparts.[115] However, there was no opportunity to do so, since Catholics believe that—in ad-dition to authorized exorcisms—prayer and the sacraments are the strongest means of fighting demons. Therefore, as they adopted the Pentecostal beliefs on other supernatural gifts, these Catholics also began imitating the Pentecostal practices of deliverance—adding certain Catholic aspects, such as asking the help of the Virgin Mary, the angels, and the saints.[116] As long as they do not claim to be performing exorcisms, they generally did not contradict Church teaching nor violate Church law.

Deliverance professionals don't violate Church law because, in the eyes of Church law, deliverance ministry does not exist. Many of them give the impression that they are Catholic experts on the subject of deliverance. Their books, websites, and organizations claim expertise on, and proficiency in performing, deliverance from demons. They even may imply that they have quasi-official accreditation or endorsement. For example, one website invites people to apply for admission to the *St. Michael Academy for Spiritual Warfare and Deliverance Counseling*, which is introduced as follows:

> In 2004, [he] founded the St. Michael Academy for Spiritual Warfare and Deliverance Counseling to provide more comprehensive training to the growing number of prospective Deliverance Counselors . . . [The founder] holds a Consilium Licentiatum Libertatis (C.L.L.), Licentiate in Deliverance Counseling, awarded on the Feast of St. Michael and the Archangels, 29 September 2004, by the St. Michael Academy for Spiritual Warfare and Deliverance Counseling, and is [a] Certified Deliverance Counselor (CDC) from that entity.[117]

Note that in the same year that this "deliverance counselor" established his academy, he also awarded himself a degree from it! This example demonstrates that since there is nothing official in the Catholic Church regarding deliverance or deliverance "ministers," individuals can create their own schools, impressive-sounding degrees with Latin names, and licensures. Looking over the websites from deliverance professionals, we see a pattern of common elements:

- Titles of authority—for example, *director* or *coordinator*—over organizations that they have usually founded and are, therefore, not associated with any Catholic diocese or religious order
- Claims of expertise in deliverance, the occult, demonology, theology, and other related fields
- Models on how to perform deliverance and run a deliverance ministry
- Claims to have expelled demons and to have healed many people from spiritual, emotional, mental, and physical problems
- Testimonials supporting miraculous healings and deliverance, but never any medical proof nor authentication by the Church
- Descriptions of talks, conferences, and seminars they conduct
- An impressive list of far-off places where they have traveled
- Books, CDs, DVDs, and other items for sale

Despite not being authorized by the Church (and some having been suppressed by the Church[118]), deliverance ministries continue to thrive and to grow in number. Some have become quite large and successful, and their leaders rich and famous.

Success Stories

Perhaps the most prominent characteristic of deliverance professionals is their stories of extraordinary spiritual powers. They claim to possess God-given knowledge of people's private lives, and insight into demonic activity. In addition, they often claim astonishing abilities to cure ailments, resolve personal problems, and heal mental disorders—all by driving out demons:

> While praying with a young woman in her twenties for some difficulties she was having, the Lord gave me a very clear word in my mind that she was having trouble with her menstrual period. I asked her about it, and she looked at me totally amazed. "How did you know?" she asked . . . As she spoke, I sensed the Holy Spirit saying to me that the problem was demonic bondage. I told the young woman that I believed she was under demonic bondage and that we should pray and command it to leave. We did so. . . . A few weeks later the woman called. She was ecstatic because she had begun her first menstrual period in eight years.[119]

Another deliverance professional describes how she healed a physical defect:

> I sensed God telling me to ask her if one of her legs was shorter than the other. . . . Sure enough, one leg was shorter. "Do you want to see a miracle?" I asked, filled with excitement. She sat down; I held her feet and began to command the short leg to grow out in the name of Jesus. About a minute later, the legs were even.[120]

The same deliverance professional tells of how she was able to expel the demons that had caused a relationship problem in her neighborhood:

> When [we] moved into this neighborhood and learned of the feud, we began to pray for a miracle of peace. First, we

told the demons involved to get out. Then we asked Jesus to cover the three houses and their families with His Precious Blood, and we prayed for this as often as we felt it was necessary. The neighbors began to treat each other like neighbors instead of enemies. The true enemy had fled.[121]

Another deliverance professional explains how he dealt with the demons instigating a child's behavior problem:

A toddler was acting aggressively and disrespectfully toward his mother one day at daily Mass. Her attempts to quiet and calm him were to no avail. You could see and sense that there was something more going on here than just a noisy toddler . . . After checking in with the Lord, I bound the spirits on the little boy. I bound spirits of disobedience and defiance and anger and malice and retaliation. Within a few seconds of completing the prayer he stretched out on the kneeler and fell asleep. He remained that way until the final blessing and then woke up at peace.[122]

He also describes fighting the demons causing a young man to hear voices and have suicidal thoughts:

The demons labeled him a "failure" and "worthless." He gave his permission to be prayed over. We bound up and cast out spirits of death, suicide, murder, lust, and pornography. Immediately a sense of peace returned to his face and to his heart . . . He now has a renewed commitment to prayer and the attacks are diminishing in their frequency and intensity.[123]

One woman was able instantly to cure her son's drug addiction:

One night her son came home in a drugged state, and when she saw him at the door in that condition, she addressed a rebuke to the demon: "Spirit of drug abuse, leave my son alone and be gone." The son staggered back as if hit by a ton of bricks and left the house. When he returned three days later, he was free of his addiction and the demon.[124]

One problem with such stories is a lack of verification. It should be easy enough for the person with one short leg to have her physician confirm that the leg suddenly lengthened. We don't know how long the neighbors were feuding, and whether the peaceful resolution lasted any length of time. Likewise, we don't know if drug-abusing son's alleged recovery was simply a typical break between binges. We certainly aren't told enough to conclude that any of these problems were demonic in origin. Addiction, depression, menstrual pains, noisy children—these things tend to have more ordinary, natural causes.

Another problem with these stories is the deliverance professionals' absolute certainty that they are receiving messages from the Holy Spirit. For example, after "checking in with the Lord," one of them could *see and sense* that the noisy toddler was being attacked by demons. People see troublesome children all the time, both inside and outside of Mass. The idea that the Holy Spirit gives people regular messages about demons involved in such mundane incidents is so absurd that it leads me to wonder about the mental health of anyone making such a claim. At a minimum, there is a bit of self-importance in the testimony of those who believe they have such familiarity with the spirit world. The same can be said of those who have devised their own means of driving out evil spirits.

COMPLEXITY OF DELIVERANCE

According to Cardinal Leon-Joseph Suenens of Brussels, "The final petition of the *Our Father*, 'Deliver us from evil,' is the supreme prayer of deliverance."[125] The deliverance professionals do not believe it is that simple. Their methods require detailed steps, specific types of prayers, and messages given to them directly from the Holy Spirit. They talk about the importance of the steps of *binding and casting out* before praying[126] and *renouncing* before the deliverance.[127] One deliverance professional gives a particular sentence that must be recited three times to break curses, spells, and hexes.[128] The same person says that during a deliverance ceremony, one member of the team should act as a lightning rod, bearing the brunt of the demonic attacks.

Needless to say, these complex methods are not found in the Bible, Church teaching, or traditional Catholic spirituality. In fact, exorcists who follow the rite (especially narrow-approach exorcists) have a simpler task dealing with cases of full possession than some deliverance professionals—with their own homespun ceremonies, prayers, and rules—have handling lower level demonic attacks.

Some of the prayers and commands typically specified by deliverance professionals include:

Prayer of Loosing

"In the name of our Lord Jesus Christ, I break all curses, spells, hexes, seals, and soul ties attached to (person's name)."[129]

Prayer of Renunciation

"In the powerful name of Jesus, I renounce any occult spirits picked up through practices that continue to harm and control me; I refuse to live under their power any longer and command them to go directly to the Foot of the Cross in the name of Jesus."[130]

Renouncing Spiritual Bondage

"In the name of Jesus I renounce the authority I gave over my life to (name of fortuneteller, soothsayer, witch, sorcerer, or wizard) and to the spirit that operated in (name)."[131]

Prayer of Taking Authority

"In the name of Jesus I break the power of every spirit that (person's name) has renounced and any related spirit, and I command them to leave now in the name of Jesus."[132]

Binding Prayer

"By virtue of my baptism and in the name, power, and authority of Jesus Christ, I bind up any and all spirits that are not of the Holy Spirit that are harassing or tempting (person's name), especially the spirits of (name the spirit)."[133]

Casting-Out Prayer

"To the degree that I have your permission, Lord, I cast out these evil spirits now in the name, power, and authority of Jesus Christ and send them immediately to the foot of the Cross to be washed in the most Precious Blood of Jesus, never to return here again. In their place Lord, I ask that you please send your Holy Spirit, your Spirit of love and truth, to fill those spaces to overflowing with your graces."[134]

Prayer of Rebuke

"In the name of Jesus, I rebuke the spirit of violence (or lust, revelry, mockery, etc.) that is present at this place. Evil spirit, I rebuke you in the name of Jesus. Be gone!"[135]

Imperative (Commanding) Prayer

"I command you, foul spirit, to leave this place (person) and go to the Foot of the Cross, now! Stop harassing the Church of God and His children. I forbid you to harm anyone or anything here, in the name of Jesus! Go, now, to the Cross!"[136]

Although there is nothing inherently wrong with these prayers, as a priest and mental health professional I think they raise several red flags. First, outside of Church rituals I am uneasy with addressing demons directly. I sense an element of pride and a need to exercise power in the desire to do so. Why not address prayers to God instead, as we do when we say *deliver us from evil* in the Lord's Prayer? In fact, in the newer Rite of Exorcism, the exorcist has the option of performing the entire ceremony without ever using imperative formulas, that is, without ever addressing demons directly.[137] This approach is a break from the traditional ceremony, and has been criticized for that reason.[138] Nevertheless, it shows that the Church believes that the exorcist can drive out demons without directly addressing them. If this is true in cases of full possession, it certainly is true that lower level assaults can be repulsed without directly addressing the evil spirits.

Furthermore, these prayers introduce unwarranted complexity to resisting the demonic. Inventing and listing categories of deliverance prayers doesn't make them more official or potent than the basic prayers and rituals of the

Church. Finally, from a mental health point of view, I fear that individuals overly concerned with demonic influences could fuel this preoccupation by talking to demons.

BOMBASTIC LANGUAGE AND UNUSUAL TERMINOLOGY

Perhaps to illustrate how worthwhile their ministry is, deliverance professionals also frequently claim to be targets for demonic antagonism:

> I cannot tell you how many times Satan has attempted to disrupt and divide my family, ministries, and prayer groups by his preemptive strikes. The days leading up to a talk I'm giving on spiritual warfare or a critical prayer meeting can be a nightmare. Seemingly out of nowhere chaos and conflict come flying at us.[139]

Notice that the language is quite dramatic: disruption, preemptive strikes, nightmares, chaos, and conflict. Contrast this with the ordinary life of any priest: he offers Mass, he preaches the gospel, he administers the sacraments. Is not such activity at least as threatening to the demons as the work of this deliverance professional? Is not the sacrifice of the Mass infinitely more threatening? Although we priests certainly believe that the devil would like to disrupt our sacramental ministry, we don't report our daily lives being affected in such a dramatic manner.

In fact, when talking about their spirituality, Catholic deliverance enthusiasts commonly use language that is atypical not only for priests but for all Catholics. One example is their frequent use of military terminology. They rightfully quote our Lord's use of such language in this Scripture: "When a strong man, fully armed, guards his own palace, his goods are in peace; but when one stronger than he assails him and overcomes him, he takes away his armor in which he trusted, and divides his spoil" (Luke 11:21–22). St. Paul used comparable martial phraseology: "Put on the whole armor of God, that you may be able to stand against the wiles of the devil . . . taking the shield of faith, with which you can quench all the flaming darts of the evil one. And take the helmet of salvation, and the sword of the Spirit, which is the word of God" (Eph. 6:11, 16, 17).

Personally, I love the imagery, and certainly I believe we are in a battle to the death with Satan and his demons. But whereas our Lord and Paul used military imagery on just a few occasions, the writings of deliverance professionals are awash in it. The phrases *spiritual warrior* and *spiritual warfare* are commonly used. Books on these topics have equally martial titles, such as *Onward Catholic Soldier, The Catholic Warrior,* and *Spiritual Warfare for Catholics.* One book has sections entitled "Tactics of the Enemy," "Basic Warfare Training," "Advanced Warfare Training," and "Ongoing Warfare Training."[140]

Catholics commonly ask God for help with their difficulties, sufferings, and sins, but deliverance enthusiasts add commands to the demons they think are responsible for these problems. As seen in some of the prayers used in their ceremonies, deliverance enthusiasts often use the phrase "spirit of ___" when addressing demons. (Sometimes they will claim that the Holy Spirit has informed them of the kind of offending spirit.) They fill in the blank with emotions such as *fear* and *anger,* sins such as *lust, fornication,* and *lies,* or peculiar names such as *blockage, games,* or *intimidation.*[141]

There are other phrases deliverance enthusiasts use that are not familiar to many Catholics in the pews, for example: sending demons to *the foot of the cross,* praying to be *covered by the Precious Blood of Christ,* and being *anointed*—not with oil, but in some more mystical way. Although there is nothing wrong with these words and phrases, those who employ them must recognize that such poetic prayer language possesses no special authority over demons. The same is true of the military terminology: those who use it should not make the mistake of thinking it gives them added spiritual power.

ARE ALL DELIVERANCE METHODS CREATED EQUAL?

Deliverance professionals tend to insist that their methods and *only* their methods, followed according to specific steps, are safe and effective at delivering people from demons. They caution against trying to perform deliverance without the proper preparation, training, and experience that they provide.

Two such professionals explain that their deliverance method is superior because it is the most comprehensive:

> Other approaches to deliverance tend to isolate one aspect of [our] approach. We do not believe that these approaches work as well as ones which integrate deliverance into a system of pastoral care . . . To isolate one stage is to risk a serious distortion or imbalance in gospel living.[142]

Another deliverance professional states that deliverance models other than his own might have some effect, but at the risk of provoking other demonic manifestations. He relates the following example of a group trying to expel demons from a woman using someone else's approach:

> The woman was blacking out and speaking with another voice, which did not respond to their commands. . . . Those praying with the woman had read a book about casting out demons. When the woman was willing to receive prayer,

they commanded the demons to leave. They got more than they bargained for. Fortunately I was able to bring the woman peace and end the session on a relatively peaceful note.[143]

Another tells the story of what can happen if the process is not done according to her model. A pastor had gone to the home of a young man named Gerard, who was a Satanist. The pastor was in the living room praying with Gerard's mother when the young man arrived.

Gerard went berserk. Screaming and swearing, he threw furniture and smashed whatever was in his reach. The well-meaning pastor did not know that his prayers for Jesus' help would anger the demons who were influencing Gerard. He did not know that binding Satan and the demons could have stopped the rampage. He did not know that casting them away from Gerard was necessary before there would even be a chance of the young man listening to him about Jesus.[144]

It should be noted that most Catholic deliverance professionals also encourage traditional Catholic spiritual practices, such as reception of the sacraments—both for those in need of deliverance and those ministering to them. They do not believe, however, that these means alone are sufficient to overcome lower level demonic attacks. Only deliverance rituals, according to the methods they have devised, will work. The reliance on gifts and messages from the Holy Spirit in discerning demonic problems is also problematic. The rite does not mention such extraordinary gifts, and as tools for discernment the American bishops' explanation mentions only "pastoral counseling, spiritual direction, [and] the Sacrament of Penance."

~

As we noted, the Catholic Church has no official deliverance doctrines, ministers, or rites. The deliverance concept, including its theology, procedures, and terminology, has been borrowed from Pentecostalism and/or invented by the deliverance professionals themselves. Prayer and the sacraments are the traditional Catholic means of fighting low-level demonic attacks. So why do Catholics need deliverance ministry?

The answer is we don't—at least not the way it is defined, explained, and practiced by the bulk of deliverance professionals and enthusiasts. Aside from rare extraordinary attacks, demons work by tempting us to sin, not by infiltrating our souls in a way that requires we be "delivered"—through techniques learned from the seminars, books, and DVDs of self-appointed experts. A sound Christian anthropology tells us that evil begins with sinful choices made by the concupiscent human will, and that we should always look for natural causes before supernatural causes. Deliverance enthusiasts, on the other hand, see demons at the heart of nearly every personal and societal problem.

Of course, as Catholics we believe we are in close contact with the spirit world. Our prayers are directed to God; we offer Mass for the souls in purgatory; we talk to our favorite saints in heaven; and we ask our guardian angels to defend us. When priests bless water, candles, medals, and other objects, they ask God to empower these holy items so that Catholics who use them will be protected from demons.

But deliverance enthusiasts say we must do more. They consider themselves spiritual warriors engaged in battle with the demonic order. Certainly, receiving messages from the Holy Spirit about attacks from evil spirits is more exciting than helping people deal with ordinary temptations.

Commanding demons to "be gone!" is more dramatic than praying the Our Father and Hail Mary. But by turning daily spiritual struggles into sensational melodramas, and by insisting that their novel prayers and rites can do what traditional Catholic spirituality cannot, deliverance enthusiasts may be doing more harm than good.

9

Good and Bad Spiritual Habits

When my brother told a friend that I had written a book on demon possession, she joked, "Is it a self-help book?" This chapter might indeed qualify as a self-help guide to resisting the influence of the devil. However, those looking for exciting rituals or dramatic commands to demons will be disappointed. With the possible exception of the Rite of Exorcism, the means of resisting the devil aren't exciting. In a certain way they are the opposite of exciting; they should contribute to a spiritual, emotional, and mental sense of peace.

We know that basic Catholic spiritual practices protect people from demonic attacks. We also know that engaging in the occult, embracing sinful lifestyles, and harboring negative emotions such as hate and revenge open doors to demons. What we do not know is why certain individuals become possessed while others who are committing worse sins do not. To draw a comparison: I have been a hospital chaplain for twelve years and have seen people afflicted with rare diseases. Although physicians cannot always explain why specific individuals contract these diseases while others do not, they do know that certain practices guard against disease in general, and they also urge people to avoid unhealthy habits.

Keep in mind that extraordinary demonic attacks are just that: extraordinary. They are so rare that even people with no spiritual life are unlikely to become possessed. Therefore, it would be false to say that one needs a good spiritual life in order to avoid demonic possession. It is the ordinary demonic attacks—everyday temptations to sin—to which people with no spiritual life are most likely to succumb. Such people are endangering their souls by having no relationship with God and following false or self-created moral teachings. Demonic possession may actually be the least of their worries! However, a faithful Catholic spiritual life is helpful in resisting both ordinary temptations and the extraordinary assaults of demons. Let us look at some practices to cultivate and to avoid if we want to keep demons at bay.

Bad Spiritual Habits

Habits—repeated practices—that make us focus on ourselves rather than God, or stoke undue curiosity about the occult, leave us more susceptible to temptation and other demonic attacks.

Emotionalism

Angels and human beings have immortal souls. Two faculties or powers of the immortal soul are reason and free will. Using our reason, we can think about things such as the morality of a proposed action. Using our free will, we can choose whether to do it. Faculties that we share with animals are senses and emotions. Our emotions are more varied and complex than those of animals, though there is no denying that a dog can be happy, sad, or angry.

We can call reason and free will *higher faculties*; emotions and senses *lower faculties*. It is a serious mistake, though one that is common in our culture, to allow the lower faculties to govern our actions. This leads us to believe that a proposed action must be good if it is pleasurable to our senses or if it makes us feel happy. I have heard individuals justify immoral acts by saying, "God wants me to be happy." This is true, but there are acts that will give us momentary pleasure but not long-term happiness. God wants us to live in eternal happiness, and to use reason rather than emotion and sensual pleasure to guide us there.

The same is true of spirituality. It is a serious mistake to think that emotions provoked during a spiritual experience indicate its depth and value. That is why, as we have seen, the Church instructs us that healing services must avoid hysteria, theatricality, and sensationalism. I have been present at such services where, despite this directive, people are encouraged to cry, make incoherent sounds, and even fall to the ground. A better spiritual experience is one that brings a sense of peace and calm, both during and afterward.

Spiritual Pride

The demons were good when God created them, but they fell from grace because of the sin of pride: "You said in your heart . . . 'I will ascend above the heights of the clouds, I will make myself like the Most High.' But you are brought down to Sheol, to the depths of the Pit" (Isa. 14:13–14). This illustrates the importance of being spiritually humble; we resist demons by avoiding the very vice that brought them down.

Spiritual Sloth

Sloth can refer to laziness in work and other daily obligations; spiritual sloth specifically refers to neglect of our obligations to God. Jesus warned us of the dangers of delaying repentance and neglecting to break our patterns of sin (Matt. 5:23–26; Luke 12:42–48). The Bible often refers to this as having a *hardened heart* (Eph. 4:18). Another way of saying this is: do not wait until tomorrow to make the good moral choices you can make today. Exorcists say that hardening of the heart, or wallowing in habits of sin, can open us to demonic attacks.

In addition to the usual spiritual means of avoiding spiritual sloth, there is a counseling technique that can be helpful in times of temptation. Before committing the sin, we can mentally put ourselves in the future and think about how we will feel about this moment. Will I be glad I acted this way, or will I regret it? What will the consequences be for others? What will the consequences be for me next week, next month, or next year? And what will the effect be on my immortal soul?

For example, if a man who struggles with drunkenness is considering having a drink, he should not dwell on the pleasure of the drink. Rather, he should mentally put himself in the future and look at what is likely to happen as a result of this one drink. If he can delay the decision to drink—if he can think about the likelihood of getting drunk, the effects on his family and other relationships/obligations, and the damage to his soul—he may be able to excite his emotions in such a way that the drink is not so desirable. These emotions counteract the pleasurable emotions that demons try to provoke in connection with our particular weaknesses. Furthermore, by developing this thought process into a habit, by God's grace we can break habits of sin that can be a door to demonic influence.

Casual Occult Practices

In artwork, the devil is often portrayed as a red creature with hooves, a pointed tail, bat wings, and a cruel smirk on his face. It would be beneficial if he actually appeared that way; it would be much easier to identify him and resist his temptations! Unfortunately, his operations are more insidious. This is also true of the occult practices that have become common in our culture. There are Catholics who would never consciously set out to worship false gods, but are lured by seemingly harmless spiritual gurus and practices that contradict the Faith. These are subtle means by which the demons try to gain a foothold and lead people away from God.

Playing with a Ouija board violates the first commandment, since it is an attempt to communicate with spirits in a way that excludes God. We can talk to angels, saints, and the souls in purgatory through their union with God, not through a board game. The only spirits that might respond to a Ouija board are demons and (possibly) human souls in hell, with neither of whom we should communicate.

Having said that, certainly many people have played with a Ouija board as children (I confess I am one of them). Many people my age have told me they did the same, and all have said they are not aware of any spiritual problems as a result. Does this mean that no harm comes from playing with a Ouija board? Definitely not, for two reasons. First, more than half of those in my generation who grew up Catholic are no longer practicing the faith. I am not blaming the Ouija board for that, but neither can we rule out the possibility that it had a negative spiritual influence on some people. Second is a comparison: when I was growing up most people were not wearing seat belts, and I didn't personally know anyone who was seriously injured or killed as a result of this neglect. Nevertheless, that does not mean it was a good idea or a safe practice.

As with the Ouija board, people who have consulted palm readers, psychics, tarot cards, and horoscopes tell me it was just for fun, and deny suffering ill effects. Certainly they did not become possessed by the devil. But these activities, too, violate the first commandment, and they have the potential of opening doors to the demonic.

As we have seen, although psychics and palm readers have no inherent ability to see the future or other hidden events, demons may use these individuals and fool their customers. Demons can put ideas in their heads, such as information about peoples' personal lives. When they report this information, they and their customers wrongly believe the knowledge came from psychic ability, palm reading or other activity. The devil would often prefer to hide his presence, and let us sin through pride (claiming extraordinary powers) and invoking false gods (such as tarot cards or the stars and planets).

Demons can also use people's grief over dead loved ones to influence them, falsely leading them to believe—through objects being moved, or lights turning off and on—that a medium has made them present in the room. But souls do not return from the dead to leave such vague and mundane signs. And demons can use such false episodes to shake people's faith in God's saving power.[145]

Ghost-busting

In chapter three we looked at the possible explanations for what are commonly called *haunted houses*. The same explanations are fitting for the phenomena called *ghosts*. If God wills it, the angels and saints in heaven can speak to people on earth. He may also send them to do good works, including carrying out his justice. He may cause them to be present in a way that can be seen. However, God would not send them to earth for the sole purpose of causing mischief: turning on lights, moving objects, or performing other trivialities just to make their presence known. Similarly, as part of their purification, God may cause souls in purgatory to perform good deeds or to give people messages. However, it is difficult to see how they would be purified simply by appearing as ghosts or causing places to seem haunted. Therefore, it is unlikely that the activities of angels, saints, or souls in purgatory could be mistaken for ghosts.

On the other hand, the demons' sole purpose is to entice us away from God. Evil spirits have the power to cause changes in the physical world. They also have the ability to appear as ghosts of deceased human beings. It makes perfect sense for demons to engage in these activities, in order to get people to pay attention to nonsense. I know Catholics who have stopped practicing their faith, but who are interested in ghosts, hauntings, and the paranormal. These are the devil's success stories. Television shows about the paranormal could be viewed solely for entertainment. However, based on the little I have seen of them, they seem to present their stories as truth rather than fiction. I strongly urge Catholics (and everyone else) not to waste time on such programs.

Popular Entertainment

Many people enjoy scary or fantastic stories. There is nothing inherently sinful about reading books and watching movies that contain ghosts, witches, vampires, or demons. But can such entertainment make us more vulnerable to demons? Many priests, including some exorcists, believe that such stories promote the dark arts, stirring up in us a curiosity about them and thereby opening doors to the demonic. These priests place such books and movies in the same category as the Ouija board, and believe media with these themes should be completely avoided. Others believe that reading or watching stories purely as fiction does not lead to an interest in the occult.

It is difficult to make a blanket statement on this topic, since so much depends on the particular stories and on the faith of the reader/viewer. Still, we should all think about the effect that these subjects of entertainment are having on our culture. Even if we can watch a particular movie on witchcraft without being influenced, it may be a good penance for us to avoid it, "to bear with the failings of the weak, and not to please ourselves" (Rom. 15:1).

GOOD SPIRITUAL HABITS

The primary purpose of all spirituality is growth in holiness, or greater union with God. Resisting the attacks of demons is a secondary effect. Another way to look at it is this: the closer we are to God, the safer we are from succumbing to demonic influence. It is important to keep our focus on God, not on the devil.

Baptism, the Eucharist, and Confession

The sacraments are the best defenses we have against demons. Baptism is the first sacrament that we receive, and is the door to receiving the other sacraments of the Church. The sacrament of baptism wipes away original sin, makes us children of God and temples of the Holy Spirit, and brings us into the Church. Baptism also is a protection against the influence of demons. Although there is disagreement among exorcists as to whether it is possible for infants and young children to be possessed by demons, most agree that they can suffer from demonic attacks, particularly if subjected to Satanism, witchcraft, or voodoo. The Code of Canon Law (no. 867) states that parents are to have their children baptized by the time they are a few weeks old. The primary reason is, of course, for the sake of the infant's eternal destiny. But early baptism has the added importance of protection against demonic attacks.

All the sacraments are powerful, but the sacraments of Holy Communion (Eucharist) and confession (the sacrament of reconciliation) are the ones that we can receive frequently. In the Eucharist, we receive the true body, blood, soul, and divinity of Christ. Furthermore, we experience union with Christ and growth in his love as a special sacramental grace. Given that the demons are separated from God forever, are incapable of love, and are filled with hatred of God and all his creatures, it is no wonder that the love of Christ we receive in the Eucharist is so powerful against their work. As St. Thomas Aquinas wrote, "It repels all the assaults of demons . . . Like lions breathing forth fire, thus do we depart from that table, being made terrible to the devil."[146]

There are several reasons why the sacrament of confession is also a powerful weapon against demonic attacks. First, it is a sacrament, and the sacraments are the most powerful channels for receiving grace, i.e. the life of Christ. Second, confession is the ordinary means by which mortal sin—a door for demonic assault—is forgiven. It also gives us the grace to resist committing those sins again. Finally, confession involves recognizing that God is the supreme lawgiver; admitting that we have disobeyed his laws, and being forgiven by him. These are experiences that the demons cannot and will not ever have. They refuse to recognize God's authority, and cannot admit that they are wrong. They will never experience the wonder of being forgiven, and hate the fact that we can.

Daily Prayer

Prayer can be defined as *lifting one's heart and mind to God*. A consistent daily prayer life is vital to overcoming the temptations of the demons, and a key to preventing their extraordinary attacks. *Consistent* is the important word here. As one exorcist said in regard to demonic possession, "It's gradual steps. No one wakes up one morning [saying], *I'm possessed*. This has all taken place over an evolution of a relationship."[147] By maintaining our daily relationship with Jesus Christ, we simultaneously avoid building a relationship with the devil. In contrast, our defenses against the demons are limited if we have an erratic prayer life. The slack times leave us more vulnerable to demonic temptations and occasions of sin.

There are two main aspects to a good daily prayer life. The first is to set aside time for prayer, preferably a regular time as part of a daily habit. The style of prayer—whether saying the rosary, Scripture reading, meditating on a crucifix, or some other method—is generally not as crucial as doing it regularly. The second aspect of daily prayer is to follow St. Paul's admonition to *pray constantly* (1 Thess. 5:17). Obviously, God does not expect us to spend most of our day in a church; not even cloistered monks and nuns do that. Rather, Paul means that we should lift our hearts and minds to God throughout the day. We can offer short prayers to God no matter where we are or what we are doing; whether we are sad or happy, stressed or relaxed, angry or having fun.

In addition to these short prayers, there is great value in having a holy image in our mind's eye. Counselors teach a form of relaxation in which a person is encouraged to picture a calming scene such as a field or stream. As Catholics, of course, we can do even better: we can picture a scene that is both calming and sacred. For example, we can imagine

Jesus, the Good Shepherd, guiding his sheep, or holding in his arms the one that had strayed. (My personal favorite is the sacred heart of Jesus; it reminds me of both the evil of my sins and the love of Christ.) The devil is capable of putting images in our minds, but he cannot force us to keep those images. The habit of having a sacred image in mind is a good defense against the sinful ideas he would like us to dwell upon.

Praying with an image in mind may have an added mental health value. There are people, of course, who struggle with anxious or obsessive thoughts. Some of these people develop a habit of repeating a prayer over and over again, especially when they are struggling with anxiety or obsessive thinking. Though I am sure God rewards them for their devotion, such prayers may not help to dispel their anxiety or obsession. However, if they can slow down their thoughts by imagining a peaceful scene with Jesus, they may have both the benefit of prayer and the calming effect of the sacred image.

Jesus said, "For where two or three are gathered in my name, there am I in the midst of them" (Matt. 18:20). We never need to pray alone, for we can always ask the intercession of the Blessed Virgin Mary, St. Joseph, St. Michael the Archangel, and any of the other angels and saints. All of them are powerful allies in defending ourselves against the temptations and attacks of demons.

Fasting

When the apostles asked why they were not able to drive the demon out of a young man, Jesus responded, "This kind cannot be driven out by anything but prayer and fasting" (Mark 9:29). In addition to prayer, fasting is a powerful weapon against demonic attack. In this regard, however, the virtue of prudence is vital. People may read stories about saints who practiced severe forms of fasting and other penances, and think they must do likewise. But I never recommend such practices. It is not severe austerity by itself that makes people into saints. Soldiers or athletes might train their bodies harshly, but this does not automatically bring them closer to Christ.

Instead, I think the best forms of penance are moderate and not noticeable to others. For example, we can follow the customary Church fast for Ash Wednesday and Good Friday: one meatless meal; no eating between meals; two small [meatless] meals only as needed to keep one's strength. Furthermore, it is best to fast in such a way that it will not be noticed by others: "But when you fast, anoint your head and wash your face, that your fasting may not be seen by men but by your Father who is in secret; and your Father who sees in secret will reward you" (Matt. 6:17). Detaching ourselves from modern conveniences and legitimate pleasures is a good form of penance. For example, we could reduce or eliminate time spent watching television or engaging in social media. The time saved might be used talking to a lonely person in need of conversation. The penance for sins, self-discipline of the body, and charity toward neighbor that these practices promote are all valuable in keeping demons at bay.

Sacramentals

Rather than words of command, extraordinary gifts, or rites of deliverance, the Church provides us with sacramentals as daily-use weapons against demons. The sign of the cross may be made devoutly, deliberately, and often; in other words, it should be *prayed*. Every home should have holy water: at night, it may be sprinkled throughout the house, and in the morning, family members can use it to make the sign of the cross. Every home should also have a crucifix—if possible, one in every room. It is also a good idea to have a crucifix in your workplace. If hanging a crucifix would get you fired, bring holy water to sprinkle discreetly around your work area—your place of employment probably needs it.

Lesser known sacramentals include blessed salt and blessed candles. I always use the extraordinary form for blessing these objects, because it specifically asks God to drive evil spirits away from those who use them. In fact, blessed salt is used in the extraordinary form of baptism. It is sprinkled on the tongue of the person being baptized while the following prayer is said: *I cast thee out, unclean spirit, in the name of the Father, and of the Son, and of the Holy Spirit. Depart from this servant of God. For it is he who commands thee, thou doomed and accursed one.* Blessed salt can be sprinkled inside or outside the home occasionally. And there is nothing wrong with sprinkling it on food! The use of blessed candles during prayer time (if it's impractical to keep one constantly lit in the home) is a good practice.

Some Christians equate sacramentals with superstition or charms. The resemblance is superficial, and ends with the fact that both are believed to have spiritual power. They are, in fact, opposites: a charm is used in an attempt to gain control over persons or things, whereas sacramentals are a recognition of God's authority over all creation. The blessings used for sacramentals make this clear, as in this beautiful prayer from the blessing of holy water:

May this creature of yours, when used in your mysteries and endowed with your grace, serve to cast out demons and to banish disease. May everything that this water sprinkles in the homes and gatherings of the faithful be delivered from all that is unclean and hurtful.

~

In this book, I have repeatedly critiqued melodramatic and over-emotional means of resisting demons. Emotion can accompany our spiritual life, but it should not be exaggerated or made the essential part. I have mentioned that other than the Rite of Exorcism, the Church's means of dealing with demons are not exciting. Perhaps I overstated that; for in a certain way the Church's methods of battling the devil are inherently exciting, so there is no need to add artificial drama.

Satan used God's creation—the forbidden fruit in the Garden of Eden—to lead our first parents to sin, so it is fitting that God uses his creation to heal us, restore us to grace, and fight back against the devil. In order to do so, the Son humbled himself and took the form of physical matter: "The Word became flesh, and dwelt among us" (John 1:14). As St. Peter said, "He went about doing good and healing all that were oppressed by the devil" (Acts 10:38). By the power of his Crucifixion, he forgives our sins and gives us his life.

The sacraments are an extension of this: God uses his material creation for the sanctification of the human race. Water washes away original sin, makes us adopted children of God, and incorporates us into the Church. Bread and wine become the body, blood, soul, and divinity of God the Son, Jesus Christ. Oil is given the power of the Holy Spirit to heal the sick, to distribute spiritual gifts in confirmation, and to confer the priesthood through holy orders. These physical channels of God's grace are powerful—and exciting—weapons in our war with the demons.

When Jesus sent forth the twelve in his name, "[He] gave them authority over unclean spirits, to cast them out, and to heal every disease and every infirmity" (Matt. 10:1). This is also a fitting description of Jesus' giving sacramentals to his Church. The sacramentals are not as powerful as the sacraments, and not directly instituted by Christ. Still, in the Bible we see their efficacy on several occasions: a woman was cured of a hemorrhage by touching Jesus' cloak; handkerchiefs that touched St. Paul were used to expel demons; and—in an Old Testament foreshadowing of a sacramental—Moses used his staff to part the Red Sea.

As beings both physical and spiritual, we have a foot in each of those realms. We have an inherent desire for physical means of conveying and expressing the power of God. The sacraments and sacramentals are Jesus' way of fulfilling this desire in our daily lives. They are also his way of taking back his creation from the dominion of the devil. The demons must think it cruel irony that, after refusing to submit to the Creator of the universe, they must now flee from a few drops of holy water, the light of a small blessed candle, or the mere sound of a consecrated church bell. This should be excitement enough for any Catholic!

Prayers for Protection
Against Demons

In their recent explanation of the Rite of Exorcism, the American bishops indicate that they plan to make available its second appendix, *Supplications which May be Used by the Faithful Privately in their Struggle against the Powers of Darkness*, as an official Church liturgical book. It will be "intended for [the general] use of the clergy and of the lay faithful in combatting the temptations of sin or spiritual attacks by the devil."

I thought it worthwhile to include a similar resource here. The following prayers are taken from official church sources, including the Mass, the Liturgy of the Hours, and the writings of the saints. Like the bishops' prayers, these are not imperative formulas that address demons directly. They are prayers asking God, his angels, and his saints to protect us against the attacks of evil spirits.

THE BLESSED VIRGIN MARY

We all know the Gospel accounts of the Blessed Virgin Mary giving birth to our Lord. We should also know that his first miracle—changing water into wine at the wedding feast in Cana—was done at her request. Jesus did not perform this miracle randomly: he was impressing upon us that the requests of his mother are very close to his heart. Less familiar than those Gospel accounts of Mary is the description of her from the book of Revelation (11:19–12:5).

Then God's temple in heaven was opened, and the ark of his covenant was seen within his temple; and there were flashes of lightning, voices, peals of thunder, an earthquake, and heavy hail. And a great portent appeared in heaven, a woman clothed with the sun, with the moon under her feet, and on her head a crown of twelve stars; she was with child and she cried out in her pangs of birth, in anguish for delivery. And another portent appeared in heaven; behold, a great red dragon, with seven heads and ten horns, and seven diadems upon his heads. His tail swept down a third of the stars of heaven, and cast them to the earth. And the dragon stood before the woman who was about to bear a child, that he might devour her child when she brought it forth; she brought forth a male child, one who is to rule all the nations with a rod of iron.

Whereas the Old Testament Ark of the Covenant contained the Ten Commandments, which were a sign of the presence of God, the Blessed Virgin is called the Ark of the Covenant because she carried within her womb God himself. The narrative from Revelation of Mary being surrounded by the sun, moon, and stars indicates why she is called the queen of heaven. Apparently it is a terrible offense to the devil's hyper-exaggerated pride that his defeat was initiated in her womb, where "the Word became flesh, and dwelt among us" (John 1:14). Several exorcists have told me it is because of the Incarnation that the demons have such hatred for the Blessed Virgin Mary.

The Rite of Exorcism states, "It will be very helpful to say devoutly over and over again the *Our Father, Hail Mary, and the Creed.*" In addition to the Hail Mary, any prayers asking for her help are valuable in resisting demonic attacks. The following hymn is from the traditional Roman Breviary for the feast of the Assumption of the Blessed Virgin Mary.

Hymn (Morning Prayer)

You are radiant in your glory, Virgin Mary, with the sun as
  your mantle,
a crown of twelve stars on your head, and the moon as
  your footstool.
Conqueror of death, hell, and sin, you now sit at Christ's
  side, ever zealous on man's behalf,
while earth and heaven sing the praises of their powerful
  queen.
But the deadly serpent still persists in his threats
  to do hurt to the people once entrusted to your care.
In your mercy, Mother, come and help us, and crush the
  head of our deadly enemy.

Blessed Virgin Mary Prayer of St. Thomas Aquinas

St. Thomas, who died in 1274, is rightfully remembered for
his brilliant teaching, but he also wrote beautiful prayers
and hymns, such as *Tantum Ergo* (Down in Adoration Falling) and *O Salutaris Hostia* (O Saving Victim). Both of these
are abbreviated versions of hymns he composed for the feast
of Corpus Christi. Here is the short form of a prayer he
wrote asking the intercession of the Blessed Virgin Mary:

O most blessed and sweet Virgin Mary, Mother of God,
  filled with all tenderness,
Daughter of the most high King, Lady of the angels,
  Mother of all the faithful,
On this day and all the days of my life, I entrust to your
  merciful heart,
my body and my soul, all my acts, thoughts, choices,
  desires, words, deeds, my entire life and death.
So that, with your assistance, all may be ordered to the good,

according to the will of your beloved Son, our Lord Jesus Christ.

Be to me, most holy Lady, a comforter,

and an ally against the stratagems and traps of the enemy

and of all those who harbor ill intentions against me.

From your beloved Son, our Lord Jesus Christ,

request for me the grace to resist firmly the temptations of the world, the flesh, and the devil,

and a constant resolve to sin no more

and to persevere in your service and the service of your Son.

I pray also that, at the end of my life, you, Mother without compromise,

Gate of Heaven and Advocate of sinners,

will not allow me, your unworthy servant, to stray from the holy Catholic faith,

But that you will protect me with your great piety and mercy, defend me from evil spirits,

and obtain for me, through the blessed and glorious Passion of your Son

and through your own intercession, received in hope, the forgiveness of all of my sins.

When I die in your love and his love,

may you direct me into the way of salvation and blessedness. Amen.

St. Joseph Hymn

The Litany of St. Joseph, approved by Pope St. Pius X, calls St. Joseph *terror of demons*. I have yet to find an explanation of this title. However, I think we can deduce several reasons from a hymn found on his feast day in the Roman Breviary. First, the demons were forced to submit to God; and as God the Son submitted himself to the authority of St. Joseph, he put the demons under Joseph. Second, Joseph was known as Jesus' father. The demons must have found it outrageous that God, who created them and banished them from heaven, allowed himself to be thought the son of a mere man, St. Joseph. Third, as the above reading from Revelation illustrates, the devil was looking for an opportunity to harm the Blessed Virgin in some way. He must have hated Joseph for being chosen by God to be Mary's earthly protector. All of these aspects of Joseph's relationship with Jesus and Mary must have been a torment to Lucifer's pride.

Joseph, glory of those in heaven, sure hope of those on
    earth, strong support of the world,
graciously accept the hymn of praise that we sing to you
    with joyful heart.
The Creator of all things appointed you the pure Virgin's
    husband,
wished you to be known as the father of the Word
and made you an instrument of man's salvation.
God, the King of kings and Lord of the world, submits
    himself to your authority,
though the power of hell trembles at his word and heaven
    adores and serves him.
Everlasting praise be to the most high Trinity that gave
    you the honors of heaven.
May we, through your merits, receive the joys of the
    blessed. Amen.

St. Joseph Prayer for the Dying

The Gospels do not record the death of St. Joseph. While the Gospels tell us that the Blessed Virgin accompanied Jesus during his public ministry, there is no mention of Joseph doing so. Therefore, it is presumed that Joseph died before the start of Jesus' earthly ministry, and that he had Jesus and Mary with him. Joseph is thus the patron saint of a happy death—which is the final triumph over the harms that demons wish to cause us. The following prayer for the dying is from the traditional rite of anointing of the sick.

To you do I turn for refuge, St. Joseph, patron of the dying,
at whose happy deathbed Jesus and Mary stood watch.
Because of this twofold pledge of hope,
I earnestly commend to you the soul of this servant, in his/
     her last agony,
so that he/she may, with you as protector, be set free from
     the snares of the devil
and from everlasting death, and may attain to everlasting joy.
Through Christ our Lord. Amen.

Novena Prayer of St. Cyriac (or Cyriacus)

St. Cyriac was a deacon of the ancient church of Rome. With his companions Largus and Smaragdus, he was martyred by the Emperor Diocletian in 303. Tradition indicates that Cyriac was a wealthy Roman noble who gave away his riches when he became a Catholic, and spent the rest of his life caring for slaves. He is also said to have driven demons out of Artemia, the daughter of Emperor Diocletian, and Jobias, the daughter of King Shapur of Persia. As a result, he has long been a patron for protection against evil spirits. His feast day is celebrated on August 8, according to the traditional liturgical calendar. Here is an ancient novena prayer asking for Cyriac's intercession:

St. Cyriac, great servant of God who loves Christ with all
     your heart,

for his sake you also loved your fellow men and served
    them even at the peril of your life.
For this charity, God rewarded you with the power to
    overcome Satan, the archenemy,
and to deliver the poor obsessed from his dreadful tyranny.
Implore for me of God an effective, real, and true charity.
Show your power over Satan also in me, and deliver me
    from his influence when he tries to tempt me.
Help me to repel his assaults and to gain the victory over
    him in life and in death.

St. Patrick's Breastplate

St. Patrick arrived on the pagan island of Ireland about 433.
By the time Patrick died thirty years later, the Faith was so
firmly established that missionaries began traveling to main-
land Europe to renew the Church there. Whether or not
Patrick actually drove snakes out of Ireland, as the pious legend goes, it is undeniable that Patrick drove out the worship
of false pagan gods and the accompanying demonic activity.

Shortly after St. Patrick arrived in Ireland, the pagans were
celebrating a high feast on the night of the Easter Vigil. Under
penalty of death, the pagan priests had forbidden anyone to
light an outdoor fire until they lit the fire for their ceremony.
Patrick and his followers ignored this command and began the
Easter Vigil Mass by lighting and blessing the Easter fire on a
hilltop. The pagan soldiers were dispatched and converged on
the hill, prepared to kill all who were taking part. However,
Patrick prayed for God's protection, and when the soldiers arrived, the Catholic worshippers appeared as a herd of deer running down the hillside. The following is part of that prayer:

I arise today through a mighty strength, the invocation of

the Trinity,
Through belief in the Three, Through confession of the
    One, the Creator of creation.
God's strength to pilot me, God's might to uphold me,
God's wisdom to guide me,
God's eye to look before me, God's ear to hear me,
God's word to speak for me,
God's hand to guard me, God's shield to protect me,
God's host to save me
From snares of devils, from temptation of vices,
From everyone who shall wish me ill, afar and near.
I summon today all these powers between me and those evils,
Against every cruel and merciless power that may oppose
    my body and soul,
Against incantations of false prophets, against black laws of
    pagandom,
Against false laws of heretics, against craft of idolatry,
Against spells of witches and smiths and wizards,
Against every knowledge that corrupts man's body and soul;
Christ to shield me today
Against poison, against burning, against drowning, against
    wounding,
So that there may come to me an abundance of reward.

St. Benedict Medal

St. Benedict started a dozen monasteries before he established
the most prominent one at Monte Cassino. Because the
rule he wrote for the monastic life has been so widely used
through the centuries, Benedict is often called the father of
Western monasticism. Benedict died in 547, and because of
his profound influence on Western civilization, is considered
one of the patron saints of Europe.

Sacred art often presents Benedict as holding a book (his rule) in one hand and a cross in the other. Over the centuries, medals came to be made with his image on one side and a cross on the other. The medals sometimes included letters that were abbreviations for prayers, possibly written by Benedict, against demons. A shattered cup and a raven were also depicted on the medals, commemorating an incident in which opponents unsuccessfully tried to murder him by adding poison to his drink and bread. When he made the sign of the cross over them, the cup shattered and a raven flew down and took away the bread. In 1880, in honor of the 1400th anniversary of Benedict's birth, the monks of Monte Cassino had a new medal designed which incorporated images from older versions. This medal has become known as the St. Benedict Medal.

There is no particular way of using the St. Benedict Medal. It may be worn around the neck, attached to a rosary, kept in a pocket, or placed somewhere in a car. It is similar to holy water in that it may also be used to ask God's blessing upon a place. For example, it may be buried in a field or yard, or placed in the foundation of a house or another building.

On the front of the medal are an image of Benedict holding his rule and a cross; a cup and a raven; the inscription *Crux S. Patris Benedicti* (Cross of Holy Father Benedict); the inscription *Ex S M Casino MDCCCLXXX* (From the Holy Mount of Cassino 1880), and the prayer *Ejus in obitu nostro presentia muniamur* (May we, at our death, be fortified by his [Christ's] presence).

A cross, the word *Pax* (Peace), and the phrase *Crux Sancti Patris Benedicti* (Cross of the Holy Father Benedict) are on the back of the St. Benedict Medal. The medal also has the Latin initials for these prayers of protection against demons:

May the Holy Cross be for me a light! (*Crux Sacra Sit Mihi Lux*)

Let not the dragon be my overlord! (*Non Draco Sit Mihi Dux*)
Begone Satan! Suggest not to me your vanities!
(*Vade retro Satana! Nunquam suade mihi vana!*)
The drink you offer is evil! Drink that poison yourself!
(*Sunt mala quae libas! Ipse venena bibas!*)

Prayer of St. Hildegard von Bingen

St. Hildegard, who died in 1170, was abbess of a monastery in Germany. Her talents are breathtaking: she excelled in theology and philosophy, musical composition, and medicine. She also had visions that she recorded in detail. In October 2012, just a few months before resigning the papacy, Pope Benedict XVI named her a Doctor of the Church. This title is given only to those saints who especially excelled in teaching. Her letters contain this prayer for help in the midst of demonic attacks:

Lord God almighty, Who in Your goodness breathed the
    breath of life into me,
I beseech you not to suffer me to be torn apart by the bit-
    terness of this great distress any longer,
but through the love of Your only begotten Son and
    Your great mercy
free me from this tribulation, and defend me from all
    the snares of the spirits of the air.
May that power which created me a man free me from
    the spirits of the air,
and may that fiery love which created me as an immortal soul,
not allow them to taint my works.

Archangels Michael, Gabriel, and Raphael

All the angels provide protection against the attacks of

demons. The archangels Michael, Gabriel, and Raphael have special roles, as they are the angels mentioned by name in the Bible. Their feast day is September 29. However, in the liturgical calendar for the traditional Mass (i.e. the Extraordinary Form), each of them had his own feast day: Michael on September 29, Gabriel on March 24, and Raphael on October 24. This hymn is from the feast of St. Michael in the traditional Roman Breviary.

Christ, glory of the holy angels, Creator and Redeemer of mankind,
grant that we may ascend to heaven to live there with the blessed.
May Michael, the angel of peace, come from heaven into our homes
bringing fair peace with him and banishing wars to hell.
May Gabriel, the angel of strength, come to banish our old enemies,
and to revisit the temples, dear to heaven,
which Christ in triumph has placed in all parts of the world.
May Raphael, the angel-physician of man's health, be with us to heal all that are sick
and to guide all who are in doubt and uncertainty.
May the virgin, queen of peace, and the mother of light, together with the holy company of angels and the radiant court of heaven ever be our help and defense.
May the blessed God, whose glory resounds through all creation, grant us this our prayer. Amen.

St. Michael

The name *Michael* means *Who is like God?* This name refers to the rebuke Michael gave to Lucifer, when the latter claimed to be like God (Isa. 14:12–15). Michael is well-known for his role in defeating Lucifer and the other angels who rebelled against God: "Now war arose in heaven, Michael and his angels fighting against the dragon; and the dragon and his angels fought, but they were defeated and there was no longer any place for them in heaven. And the great dragon was thrown down, that ancient serpent, who is called the Devil and Satan, the deceiver of the whole world—he was thrown down to the earth, and his angels were thrown down with him" (Rev. 12:7–9). The epistle of Jude (1:9) refers to a mysterious dispute Michael had with the devil: "But when the archangel Michael, contending with the devil, disputed about the body of Moses, he did not presume to pronounce a reviling judgment upon him, but said, 'The Lord rebuke you.'" In the book of the prophet Daniel, Michael is called the prince of the people of Israel (10:13, 12:1). The Extraordinary Form Mass invokes Michael at the blessing of incense during the offertory:

Through the intercession of Blessed Michael the Archangel, standing at the right hand of the altar of incense, and of all His elect, may the Lord vouchsafe to bless this incense and to receive it in the odor of sweetness.

As Michael was the leader of the angels who cast the evil spirits out of heaven, he is also a powerful ally in our battle against the wickedness and snares of the devil. The following collect or opening prayer is from the feast of St. Michael; the hymn is from the traditional Roman breviary:

PRAYER

O God, who dispose in marvelous order ministries both angelic and human, graciously grant that our life on earth may be defended by those who watch over us as they minister perpetually to you in heaven.

Hymn (Evening Prayer)

Jesus, the radiance and power of the Father and life of all
    hearts,
we offer You our praise in company with the Angels who
    ever wait on Your wishes.
An army of thousands upon thousands in close array fights
    for Your cause,
but Michael, their victorious leader and the standard-bearer
    of salvation,
unfurls the standard of the cross.
He casts the wicked dragon into the depths of hell
and hurls Satan and his rebel followers like lightning from
    high heaven.
Let Michael be our leader in the battle with the prince of pride
that the lamb, enthroned in heaven, may reward us with
    the crown of glory.
Glory be to God the Father.
May he guard through his Angels those whom the Son has
    redeemed
and the Holy Spirit has anointed. Amen.

St. Gabriel

The name *Gabriel* means *God's strength*. In the Old Testament, Gabriel interpreted visions for the prophet Daniel (Dan. 8:16, 9:21). In the New Testament, he told the priest Zechariah that his wife Elizabeth would bear a son in her old age. This child, St. John the Baptist, would prepare the way for the Messiah. Gabriel's most important role, of course, was the announcement to the Blessed Virgin Mary that she was to be the mother of Jesus, the Messiah (Luke 1:26–38). This was the death-blow to Lucifer's reign on earth. We can ask Gabriel to strengthen us as we do our part in battling the devil. Here is a prayer from the Extraordinary Form Mass collect for Gabriel's feast day:

> O God, who did choose from among all other angels the archangel Gabriel to announce the mystery of your Incarnation, grant in your mercy that celebrating his feast on earth, we may reap the effect of his protection in heaven.

St. Raphael

The name *Raphael* means *God heals*. The archangel Raphael played the key role in the Old Testament book of Tobit, as a guide for Tobit's son Tobias. Raphael helped to arrange the marriage of Tobias to Sarah, whose seven previous husbands had been murdered on their wedding night by the demon Asmodeus (the Destroyer). On the night that Tobias and Sarah were married, Raphael pursued Asmodeus into the desert and bound him there. Raphael accompanied the young couple back to Tobias's home, healed Tobit's blindness, and finally revealed his identity: "I am Raphael, one of the seven holy angels who present the prayers of the saints and enter into the presence of the glory of the Holy One" (Tob. 12:15). For obvious reasons, people look to Raphael for help in finding a good husband or wife, as well as for protection from demonic attacks. This is his feast day collect from the Mass in the Extraordinary Form:

> O God, who to Tobias, your servant, when on his journey, did give blessed Raphael the archangel as a companion,

grant to us, your servants, that we be ever protected by his custody and strengthened by his help.

Holy Guardian Angels

The Catechism of the Council of Trent (Part IV) gives the following description of the role of our guardian angels in protecting us from the devil:

> In the journey we are making towards our heavenly country our heavenly Father has placed over each of us an Angel under whose protection and vigilance we may be enabled to escape the snares secretly prepared by our enemy, repel the dreadful attacks he makes on us, and under his guiding hand keep the right road, and thus be secure against all false steps which the wiles of the evil one might cause us to make in order to draw us aside from the path that leads to heaven.

Someone once asked me, "Why do we need guardian angels? God can protect us himself." That is certainly true, and I have no answer to the question. Neither do I know *why* God created the universe, for he is infinitely happy in himself and has no need of anything. However, somehow the existence and ministry of guardian angels fit in his plan and glorify him. Personally, I find it very reassuring to know that I have an angel whose mission is to protect me from spiritual harm. The Bible has many stories of angels protecting God's faithful people and carrying out his justice against his enemies. An angel guided the Israelites out of Egypt and protected them from the Egyptians' pursuit (Ex. 14:19). An angel freed Peter from his chains and led him out of prison (Acts 12:1–19). In warning his disciples not to scandalize children, Jesus said, "See that you do not despise one of these little ones; for I tell you that in heaven their angels always behold the face of my Father who is in heaven" (Matt.18:10).

I find it mysterious and fascinating that angels can be on earth helping us while at the same time seeing the face of God in heaven. Thomas Aquinas said that when the demons are here on earth assaulting us, demons are still suffering the pains of hell, for they carry hell with them.[148] The opposite is true of the angels: even while here on earth protecting us, angels are still experiencing the glory of heaven, for they carry heaven with them.

We should take time each day to ask the help of our guardian angels and to thank God for sending them to us. Throughout the day, any time that we must endure suffering, face difficulties or danger, or resist temptation, we should pause to ask our guardian angel for help. Obviously, we should pray to God in all of these circumstances, but it is fitting also to look to our angel guardians. After all, though God could have banished Lucifer and the demons from heaven by his own divine power, God willed to do so through his angels. The angels continue to guard us against the demons who afflict us in our daily lives.

This prayer is the post-Communion prayer from the Extraordinary Form Mass on the feast of the Guardian Angels; the hymns are from the traditional Roman Breviary.

PRAYER

We have received your divine mysteries, O Lord, in joyful celebration of the feast of thy holy angels; we beseech thee, that by their protection, we may always be safe from the wiles of our enemies and guarded from all harm. Amen.

HYMN (OFFICE OF READINGS)

We sing of the Angels, guardians of men,
that the heavenly Father has given as an additional help to
    our weak nature,
that it may not yield to enemies ever ready to attack.
For since the traitor angel fell headlong to his destruction
and was rightly deprived of honors that once were his, he
    has been on fire with envy
and endeavoring to hurl to their destruction those that
    God is inviting to heaven.
Therefore fly to us here, ever-watchful guardian,
and ward off from the land entrusted to your care
all spiritual illness, and everything that denies its people
    peace of soul.
Loving praise be forever given to the Holy Trinity,
whose power rules the threefold fabric of the world
and whose glory and kingdom last for all eternity. Amen.

HYMN (EVENING PRAYER)

Eternal ruler of the stars, with mighty power you created
and with no less mighty providence you rule all that is.
Listen to us sinners, here gathered together, as we pray to you.
The light of day is now fading; grant new light to our souls.
May your angel that was chosen as our guardian
be present here to protect us from sin's contamination.
May he keep far from us the wily and envious devil
that our unwary hearts be not ensnared in the net of his
    deceitfulness.
May he take from our land all fear of invasion,
be the cause of peace amongst its inhabitants, and banish
    plague and disease.
Glory be to God the Father. May he guard through his angels

those whom the Son has redeemed and the Holy Spirit has anointed. Amen.

GUARDIAN ANGEL PRAYER OF ST. GERTRUDE

St. Gertrude, who died in 1302, was from Saxony, a region of present-day Germany. She became a nun and eventually abbess of her monastery. Gertrude was known for her meditations on our Lord's Passion, her devotion to the Eucharist, and her love of the Blessed Virgin Mary. Here is a prayer she wrote to her guardian angel:

O most holy angel of God, appointed by God to be my
    guardian,
I give you thanks for all the benefits which you have ever
    bestowed on me in body and in soul.
I praise and glorify you that you condescended to assist me
    with such patient fidelity,
and to defend me against all the assaults of my enemies.
Blessed be the hour in which you were assigned me
for my guardian, my defender and my patron.
In acknowledgement and return for all your loving minis-
    tries to me,
I offer you the infinitely precious and noble heart of Jesus,
and firmly purpose to obey you henceforward, and most
    faithfully to serve my God. Amen.

SUNDAY NIGHT PRAYER

Finally, here is a night prayer for Sunday from the Liturgy of the Hours. It seems an appropriate way to conclude this book:

Lord, we beg you to visit this house and banish from it all

the deadly power of the enemy. May your holy angels dwell here to keep us in peace, and may your blessing be upon us always. We ask this through Christ our Lord. Amen.

Appendix II

Advice for Pastors and Ministers

What can pastors and clergy, retreat-leaders, and others engaged in ministry learn from the Gospel stories of Jesus' dealings with demons? I think they are instructive on several points.

1. Jesus and the apostles drove out demons on many occasions, but only a few times is there mention of a type of demon. The phrases *spirit of infirmity*, *deaf and dumb spirit*, and *clairvoyant spirit* indicate the effect that each demon had on its victim (Matt.17:14–21; Luke 13:10–16; Acts 16:16–18). Other than on those occasions, the New Testament does not mention different types of demons; neither does the Rite of Exorcism mention such categories. In contrast, deliverance professionals and exorcists who follow the wide approach to exorcism have established numerous categories and types of demons. Although there is nothing absolutely wrong with this aspect of the wide approach, it is unnecessary in expelling demons, and over-emphasized in the writings of these exorcists.

2. Jesus' parable of the man sowing seeds (Matt. 13:1–23) is helpful for putting demonic attacks in perspective. The seeds that fell on the path were eaten by birds; those on rocky ground sprang up at once, but were withered by the sun because of their lack of roots; some fell amongst thorns and were choked by them; but those that fell on good soil grew and yielded abundant fruit. Jesus explained that the seeds taken by the birds are people who are stolen by the

devil; the seeds on rocky ground are those who fall away in times of suffering or persecution; the seeds choked by weeds are those overcome by anxiety and greed of worldly things; and the seeds on good soil are people who hear his word and understand, and thereby bear fruit.

Note that the devil is one cause of infidelity, but there are other causes, too. Therefore, although the devil did bring evil into the world at the beginning, and demons always wish to tempt us to sin, we should not attribute all evils to them.

3. Jesus did say that those who believe in him would drive out demons in his name (Mark 16:17–18). In these same verses he also said, however, that believers would speak new languages, pick up serpents with their hands, drink poison without being harmed, and cure the sick by laying hands on them. Clearly he did not mean that every one of his followers—or even many of them—would take part in every one of these miraculous activities. It may be the case that driving out demons is almost as rare as drinking poison without being harmed.

4. After Jesus drove the legion of demons from the Gerasene man, the Gospel says that the people saw the man *in his right mind.* This suggests that the man may have been mentally ill as well as demon-possessed, and that Jesus healed him of both problems. Exorcists agree that it is common for people who are victims of demonic possession, obsession, and oppression to be suffering from mental disorders as well. The mental disorders may be caused by the demons, in which case expelling them will also heal the mental problems. However, this is not always the case; the mental disorders may be present independent of the demonic attacks. Demons are evil, and therefore enjoy attacking

our weaknesses. They may attack individuals with mental disorders and make their problems worse.

Counsel for Clergy

With these examples of Jesus as a starting point, how can Catholic clergy put the matter of demonic attacks into context for their flock? I will offer some suggestions.

Traditional Spirituality

The clergy should stress the importance of Mass, the sacrament of penance, daily prayer, the corporal and spiritual works of mercy, and avoiding near occasions of sin. Similarly, bishops, priests, and deacons should encourage the use of sacramentals: keeping holy water containers full in church vestibules, offering to bless medals, statues, and rosaries, blessing homes when on sick calls or other parish visits, and (of course) blessing people at every opportunity.

As a hospital chaplain, I carry holy water at all times and sprinkle it on patients whose condition does not warrant the anointing of the sick. I frequently have occasion to give the blessing for expectant mothers; it imparts God's grace to both the mother and her child, and it impresses on those present the reality of the life that she carries within her womb. When blessing homes, I prefer the traditional blessing, because it specifically asks God to send an angel to protect all who live there.

Deliverance

Because there are no appointed positions, liturgical ceremonies, or official Church methods, deliverance is the Wild West of demon-fighting. Anyone can claim expertise in demonology and deliverance. The percentage of the clergy involved in this is small, and I am fairly certain that if any of them were to read my advice, they would heartily disagree with it. I hope for a better hearing from bishops, and from priests and deacons not involved in deliverance ministry.

The clergy should certainly pray with and for individuals who think they are being attacked by demons. If this is called *deliverance*, that's fine. The problem arises when *deliverance ministers*—whether clergy or laity—claim to have special prayers, methods, and spiritual gifts that make them especially proficient in fighting demons. Compounding the problem is their practice of advertising deliverance prayer services in order to attract crowds. I ask bishops to consider putting some of the same restrictions on so-called *deliverance* that are in place for exorcisms: prohibiting them from being advertised, publicized, or video recorded, and from being done in conjunction with healing services; and requiring that there be only a few people present (to assist the priest or deacon).

Bishops might also consider promulgating a small *deliverance manual* for use by both clergy and laity. A deliverance manual could include instruction on the topic, Scripture readings, prayers written by saints, prayers from the Mass, and blessings from the Roman Ritual that specifically drive away demons. Saints such as Patrick, Thomas Aquinas, and Hildegard von Bingen wrote prayers asking God for protection from demons; these could be included. I believe that a ritual backed by the authority of the bishop, and specifically intended for the purpose of fighting demonic attacks, may indeed be very effective in doing so.

Healing services

Healing service is the generic name given to gatherings of

Catholics for the specific purpose of—quite obviously—praying for healing. As with deliverance ministry, the Church has no appointed position or office for a person to be a healer, and there is no official Church method of performing such services. There are Catholic healing services that are calm events, conducive to physical, mental, emotional, and spiritual healing. Unfortunately, there are also healing services, led by self-proclaimed *healing priests*,[149] that are rampant with emotionalism. Mentally fragile people do not benefit from spiritual activities that deliberately inflame their emotions.

In order to regulate these proceedings, in the year 2000 the Sacred Congregation for the Doctrine of the Faith issued *Instruction on Prayers for Healing*. Approved by Pope John Paul II, it attempted to regulate healing services, and included the following directives.

- In gatherings organized for the purpose of praying for healing, it is inappropriate to attribute a gift of healing to any category of participants; for example, to the directors of the group.
- Anything resembling hysteria, artificiality, theatricality, or sensationalism, above all on the part of those who are in charge of such gatherings, must not take place.
- The Rite of Exorcism must not be performed in conjunction with healing services.

Deliverance professionals may work around the latter restriction by claiming to drive out demons through deliverance rather than exorcism. The result is that, on one hand, they would not be directly contradicting Church doctrine or violating Church law in this regard. But on the other hand, they give the impression that they are performing a Church ceremony that has special power to drive out demons. Similarly, they often encourage the idea that *laying hands on* people and praying *over* them is somehow more efficacious than *folding* one's hands and praying *for* them.

As a more traditional and less emotional alternative, parishes could have a monthly or quarterly healing service consisting of Mass, Exposition of the Blessed Sacrament, devotions to a patron saint, and the opportunity to receive the sacraments of penance and anointing of the sick. Rather than looking to individuals claiming special healing abilities, Catholics should incorporate devotions to the saints in calm and prayerful healing services. St. Blaise for diseases of the throat, St. Denis for headaches, St. Peregrine for cancer, St. Eustace for family troubles, St. Dymphna for mental and emotional disorders, St. Margaret of Antioch for demon assaults, and St. Jude for all manner of hopeless causes, are just a few of the numerous saints whom Catholics have traditionally asked for assistance for physical, mental, and spiritual problems.

Retreats and renewals

The same advice for deliverance ministry and healing services is valid for all retreats, renewals, or spiritual programs: they should not encourage excessive emotional arousal of those attending. People who are struggling emotionally are precisely those who are most likely to think the emotional high they receive is actually a spiritual experience. The inevitable emotional letdown that occurs after the retreat or renewal leaves them feeling spiritually abandoned. Some of them continually search for such programs in order to feed the emotional high. In contrast, a solid retreat or renewal will help instill in them a sense of calm and spiritual peace, with the goal of enabling them to continue this on their own.

There are several steps that the leaders can take to prevent people from becoming hyper-emotional, rather than encouraging it. For example, at overnight gatherings, there should be rules about turning off the lights and keeping silence for eight hours at night. Sleep deprivation does not lead to deep spiritual experiences, but instead contributes to physical, mental, and emotional exhaustion. In addition, participants should be given the schedule at the start. In our time-focused culture, it is disorienting for people to suddenly have no schedule and no idea of the time. The practice of not giving participants a schedule—and in some cases, not letting them see clocks or their watches—is more likely to raise anxiety than to give a sense of spiritual peace.

In regard to the program itself, the emphasis should be on spiritual talks rather than personal sharing. Groups of strangers exchanging details of their private lives leads to a false sense of intimacy, especially if done for an entire weekend. Leaders should also keep in mind that the importance of avoiding excessive emotionalism increases when it comes to teenagers. Adults should never deliberately attempt to arouse teenagers' emotions. They do a good job of it without our help!

COUNSEL FOR EXORCISTS

At the risk of sounding presumptuous, I would like to offer some counsel to my brother priests who perform exorcisms, and to the bishops who appoint them. Though not an exorcist, I hope that having a degree in mental health counseling—and having extensively researched its relationship to possession and exorcism—qualifies me to give some advice from a professional standpoint.

Diagnostic Exorcisms

The 1999 Rite of Exorcism requires the exorcist to have the moral certitude that individuals are possessed before he performs the exorcism ritual.[150] This rules out the so-called *diagnostic exorcism*, or the performance of the rite in order to learn whether or not individuals are possessed. Although the 1614 Rite of Exorcism does not give this instruction, it seems a prudent addition, and it is reinforced by the explanation given by the American bishops.[151] For the sake of the mental health of troubled individuals, exorcists should refrain from performing exorcisms unless and until they have such certitude; otherwise, there may be detrimental consequences of unnecessary exorcisms.

Symptoms of mental disorders

As we have seen, the wide approach takes into account many signs in addition to the three from the Rite of Exorcism. The Bible tells us that demons can indeed cause such signs, but we know the signs can also be the result of natural causes. This demonstrates the value of relying on the three extraordinary signs found in the Rite of Exorcism. When these are present, we can be reasonably certain that demons are involved. When the other symptoms are present but the three signs are not, it is likely to be a mental disorder. Exorcists should not perform exorcisms in cases that can be explained by natural causes.

Serious mental disorders are typically accompanied by relationship problems, financial difficulties, and physical health problems (due to lack of self-care). Exorcists who look at all of these as potential signs of possession should consider that they may instead be seeing the common, tragic results of serious mental disorders. In those rare cases where the three signs from the Rite of Exorcism are also present, demonic attack may be to blame for all of these evils.

One wide approach exorcist says that the observed signs and experiences of demon possession vary from one exorcist to another.[152] As an example, he says that he often sees pains in the head and stomach as signs of possession, whereas other exorcists do not. This raises a difficulty, since it would suggest that demons behave differently when in the presence of different exorcists. One explanation is that this is in fact the case, and the demons do so deliberately to cause confusion, especially among the exorcists who are attempting to expel them. However, another explanation is that these alleged signs of possession are actually symptoms of physical, mental, and/or emotional disorders. In either case, the prescription is the same: if individuals manifest the signs from the rite, the exorcist should proceed with the exorcism; if not, he should refer them for physical and/or mental health assessments.

Duration of exorcisms

Another indication that a problem may not be demonic is when an exorcist is unsuccessful, despite performing many exorcism sessions over the course of many months. One exorcist said that he receives cases where years of counseling sessions did not resolve the individuals' problems, but he is able to do so by performing exorcisms. Yet the same exorcist says that some cases of possession are not resolved despite many exorcism sessions over the course of years. Instead of concluding that these individuals are not actually possessed, he considers them to be difficult cases. This would be understandable if the individual were manifesting the three signs from the rite for that length of time. However, if the exorcist is basing his evaluation on the other signs, it is likely the problem is mental rather than demonic.

Claims of Extraordinary Gifts

Some exorcists rely on the assistance of people claiming to have spiritual gifts that enable them to sense the presence and activity of demons. This ability, sometimes called *discernment of spirits*, is rare even among the saints; and even they have had difficulty determining "when the action of God terminates and when the natural or diabolical movement begins."[153] Yet those who follow Pentecostal spirituality, and Catholics who have borrowed some of their ideas, allege this infused ability to be relatively common, and believe extraordinary spiritual gifts occur frequently.

It would be a serious mistake for exorcists to rely on these individuals to help distinguish between demonic attacks and mental disorders. The rite says nothing about this practice, and exorcists who follow the narrow approach seem to do fine without allegedly gifted individuals. Again, the solution is to look for the three signs from the rite. If they are present, there is no need for extraordinary spiritual gifts; if the signs are not present, the exorcist should look for natural causes for the condition. More common and more useful than this supernatural gift is the natural ability of a spiritual director to assist in discerning whether particular decisions are from God, the devil, or the human person. This ability is developed through prayer, study, experience, and good moral character.[154]

Consequences of Unnecessary Exorcisms

"An unnecessary exorcism never harmed anyone," claims one exorcist. However, another exorcist opposes this idea:

"The Rite of Exorcism is like a nuclear bomb. It's in our arsenal but that doesn't mean we use it all the time. That's the last resort."Needless to say, the first exorcist follows the wide approach, while the second uses the narrow approach. The American bishops support the latter in their recent explanation of the topic. They recommend that each diocese have a protocol for determining demonic possession, in order to ensure that caution is exercised and to prevent "a sensationalist mentality and . . . a kind of sideshow affair."[155]

As a mental health counselor, I believe a number of negative consequences may arise from performing unnecessary exorcisms:

- Those with mental disorders often feel a lack of control over their emotions, thoughts, and behaviors. If they are truly possessed, they will regain control through a successful exorcism. If they are not possessed, an unnecessary exorcism can reinforce the belief that they have no control in these areas.
- Mentally disturbed individuals sometimes sense an evil presence in or near them. In cases of true possession, a successful exorcism can resolve this. However, a wrong diagnosis and an unnecessary exorcism can leave them feeling that even an exorcist cannot drive out the evil presence they believe is afflicting them.
- There are psychological studies on the effect of exorcisms on mental health. One involved fifteen people with dissociative identity disorder (or multiple personality disorder) who agreed to undergo exorcisms.[156] Most of them later disagreed with the idea that they were demon-possessed, were angry about the experience, and had a more negative view of religion as a result of it. Some became suicidal and had to be hospitalized after the exorcisms.

- Individuals with dissociative identity disorder are believed to have a number of different personalities as a result of trauma and abuse. Psychological treatment for this disorder involves gradually helping them to realize that these identities are all part of the same individual person. In the course of a mistaken and unnecessary exorcism, the exorcist might repeatedly address these different personalities as different demons. In doing so, he would reinforce the idea that they are different persons, and make the disorder even more ingrained.
- If an exorcist wrongly convinces people they are possessed by demons, these individuals may be less likely to follow through with the mental health therapy they need.

~

Catholic bishops, priests, and deacons see Jesus as the model for the range of their pastoral ministry. This includes following his example in the way he healed those suffering from illnesses as well as demonic attacks. Our Lord did not see demons as the only—or even the primary—source of sin; he distinguished between ordinary sickness and demon possession; and he tried to avoid crowds when performing his healings and exorcisms.

When it comes to dealing with demonic issues, Catholic clergy as well as lay ministers should follow Jesus' example. We must not put too much emphasis on the demonic; it is important to address the temptations of the flesh and the world that are rampant in our culture. We must be careful to assist the suffering in getting the help they need, whether it be physical, mental, or spiritual. Finally, we should perform our ministry as quietly and humbly as possible. There is no need to have large numbers of people present when we are performing some private ministry to individuals. Try to get the crowds for Mass and confession!

About the Author

Fr. Mike Driscoll is a priest of the Diocese of Peoria, Illinois. He was ordained in 1992, has been pastor of several parishes, and is currently serving as chaplain of St. Elizabeth's Medical Center in Ottawa, Illinois. He has a B.A. in economics from the University of Illinois, an M.A. in moral theology from Mount St. Mary's Seminary, and a Ph.D. in counselor education and supervision from Regent University. His book of short stories, *The Fr. Capranica Mysteries,* is published by Bezalel Books. He can be contacted through his website: peterinchains.org.

Notes

1.   Erika Bourguignon, "Introduction: A Framework for the Comparative Study of Altered States of Consciousness," in *Religion, Altered
     States of Consciousness, and Social Change*, ed. by Erika Bourguignon
     (Columbus, OH: Ohio State University Press, 1973), 3–35.

2.   Felicitas Goodman, *The Exorcism of Anneliese Michel* (Eugene,
     OR: Resource Publications, 1981), 201–226.

3.   The Bible and the Church offer no teaching on the existence
     of extraterrestrials created in God's image; that is, having immortal souls.

4.   Belief in *limbo* is a theological opinion, not a Church teaching,
     so I am not addressing it here.

5.   Morton Klass, *Mind Over Mind* (Lanham, MD: Rowman & Littlefield, 2003), 41–43.

6.   Peter Claus, "The Siri Myth and Ritual: A Mass Possession Cult
     of South India," *Ethnology*, 14, no. 1 (Jan. 1975), 47–58.

7.   Kenneth Stewart, "Possession in Native America," *Southwestern
     Journal of Anthropology* 2, no. 3 (Autumn 1946), 323–339.

8.   Takawira Kazembe, "'Divine Angels' and Vadzimu in Shona
     Religion, Zimbabwe," *Rose-Croix Journal* 8 (2011), 89–98.

9.   Lafcadio Hearn, *Glimpses of Unfamiliar Japan* (North Clerndon,
     VT: Periplus, 1976/209), 253–280.

10. Karen Smyers, *The Fox and the Jewel: Shared and Private Meanings
     in Contemporary Japanese Inari Worship* (Honolulu: University of
     Hawaii, 1999), 76–96.

11. Hearn, *Glimpses*, 253–280.

12. Goodman, *The Exorcism*, 206–208.

13. Klass, *Mind Over Mind*, 48.

14. Felicitas Goodman, *How About Demons?* (Bloomington, IN:
     University of Indiana, 1988), 111.

15. Aubrey Parke, "The Qawa Incident in 1968 and Other Cases

of 'Spirit Possession,'" *Journal of Pacific History* 30, no. 2 (1995), 210–226.

16. Patrick McNamara, *Spirit Possession and Exorcism: History, Psychology, and Neurobiology, Volume 2: Rites to Become Possessed, Rites to Exorcize "Demons"* (Santa Barbara, CA: Praeger, 2011), 99–104.

17. Heather Kavan, "The Korean Exorcist Meets the New Zealand Justice System," *Aotearoa Ethnic Network Journal* 2, no. 2 (August 2007), 53–58.

18. Goodman, *How About Demons*, 89–93.

19. *Summa Theologica*, I, 61, 1.

20. Ibid., 64, 110–111.

21. Ibid., 64, 4.

22. Mike Driscoll, "*How Catholic Exorcists Distinguish between Demonic Possession and Mental Disorders*" (Ph.D. diss. Regent University, 2013), 86.

23. Ibid., 88.

24. USCCB, http://www.usccb.org/prayer-and-worship/sacraments-and-sacramentals/sacramentals-blessings/exorcism.cfm.

25. Jordan Aumann, *Spiritual Theology* (London: Sheed & Ward, 1980), 419–421.

26. Munroe Falls Paranormal Society, http://www.munroe-falls-paranormal-society.com/blog/?p=222.

27. Additional signs of possession named in this chapter are taken from the following sources: Gabriele Amorth, *An Exorcist Tells His Story*, trans. Nicoletta MacKenzie (San Francisco: Ignatius Press, 1999), 67–116. Jordan Aumann, *Spiritual Theology* (London: Sheed & Ward, 1980), 399–441. Corrado Balducci, *The Devil: Alive and Active in Our World*, trans. Jordan Aumann (New York: Alba House, 1990), 109–151. Leon Cristiani, *Evidence of Satan in the Modern World*, trans. Cynthia Rowland (Rockford, IL: TAN Books, 1974), 62–73. Mike Driscoll, "*How Catholic Exorcists Distinguish between Demonic Possession and Mental Disorders*" (Ph.D. diss. Regent University, 2013), 109–167. Thomas Eute-

neuer, *Exorcism and the Church Militant* (Front Royal, VA: Human Life International, 2010), 97–125. José Fortea, *Interview with an Exorcist* (West Chester, PA: Ascension Press, 2006), 65–123.

28. Driscoll, *How Catholic Exorcists,* 210.

29. Morton Hunt, *The Story of Psychology* (New York: Anchor, 2007), 17–19.

30. American Psychiatric Association, *Diagnostic and Statistical Manual of Mental Disorders, Fifth Edition* (Arlington, VA: American Psychiatric Association, 2013).

31. Ibid., 298–299.

32. Flora Schreiber, *Sybil* (New York: Warner Books, 1973).

33. Robert Rieber, "Hypnosis, False Memory and Multiple Personality: A Trinity of Affinity," *History of Psychiatry* 10, no. 37 (March 1999), 3–11.

34. Mark Lawrence, "Review of Bifurcation of the Self: The history and theory of dissociation and its disorders," *American Journal of Clinical Hypnosis* 50, no. 3 (May 2010), 273–283.

35. John Kihlstrom, "Dissociative Disorders," *Annual Review of Clinical Psychology* 1 (April 2005), 227–253.

36. Goodman, *How About Demons,* 79–86.

37. Deborah Haddock, *The Dissociative Identity Disorder Handbook* (New York: McGraw-Hill, 2001), 212–216.

38. APA, *DSM–5*, 87–122.

39. Ibid., 783–786.

40. Ibid., 87.

41. Ibid., 155–188.

42. Ibid., 309–327.

43. American Psychiatric Association, *Diagnostic and Statistical Manual of Mental Disorders, Fourth Edition, Text Revision* (Arlington, VA: American Psychiatric Association, 2000), 485–511.

44. APA, *DSM–5*, 649–652.

45. Millon, *Masters of the Mind*, 42–80; Roy Porter, *Madness: A Brief History* (Oxford: Oxford University, 2002), 62–122.

46. We need not look to the Middle Ages to find poor treatment of the mentally ill. To cite a recent example, an internal review of North Carolina's Central Prison found that mentally ill inmates in so-called *therapeutic seclusion* were isolated for weeks, with no clothing or mattresses, in cells described as being infested with roaches and human waste. Individual cases of abuse of the mentally ill, whether by the ancient Catholic Church or present-day mental health therapists, should not be presumed to be standard practice.

47. See Herbert Thurston and Donald Attwater, eds., *Butler's Lives of the Saints* (Westminster, MD: Christian Classics, 1981).

48. In November 2014, the American bishops approved an English translation of the new rite, and submitted it to the Vatican for approval.

49. *Compendium of the Catechism of the Catholic Church*, 224.

50. Ibid., 351.

51. Driscoll, *How Catholic Exorcists,* 240.

52. Jeffrey S. Grob, "A major revision of the discipline on exorcism: a comparative study of the liturgical laws in the 1614 and 1998 rituals" (Canon Law diss., St. Paul University, Ottawa, Canada, 2007), 41–101.

53. USCCB, http://www.usccb.org/prayer-and-worship/sacraments-and-sacramentals/sacramentals-blessings/exorcism.cfm. The bishops' committee plans to publish this appendix separately, once the English translations have been approved by the Vatican.

54. *Praenotanda*, section 16.

55. Driscoll, *How Catholic Exorcists,* 94.

56. USCCB, http://www.usccb.org/prayer-and-worship/sacraments-and-sacramentals/sacramentals-blessings/exorcism.cfm.

57. Euteneuer, *Exorcism*, 169.

58. Driscoll, *How Catholic Exorcists,* 263.

59. Ibid., 314.

60. Fortea, *Interview with an Exorcist*, 100–101.

61. Diocese of Springfield, website. http://www.dio.org/blog/

item/350-bishop-paprocki-s-homily-for-prayers-of-supplication-and-exorcism-in-reparation-for-the-sin-of-same-sex-marriage.html#sthash.K92ycAGq.dpbs.

62. The recent USCCB explanation of the rite, however, states: "It is also strongly suggested that the identity of the exorcist be kept secret or at most known only to the other priests of the diocese so as not to overwhelm the exorcist with random calls and inquiries."

63. Driscoll, *How Catholic Exorcists*, 230–231.

64. Ibid., 129.

65. Ibid., 88.

66. Ibid., 89.

67. Ibid., 135.

68. Ibid., 131, 155.

69. Thomas Allen, *Possessed* (iUniverse.com, 1994), 37–38.

70. Driscoll, *How Catholic Exorcists*, 130.

71. Ibid., 155.

72. Ibid., 81.

73. Ibid., 159–160.

74. Ibid.

75. Ibid.

76. Ibid., 76.

77. Unless otherwise noted, descriptions of the narrow approach are from Driscoll, *How Catholic Exorcists*, 109–167. Descriptions of the wide approach are from Amorth, *An Exorcist*, 67–116; Euteneuer, *Exorcism*, 97–125; Fortea, *Interview with an Exorcist*, 65–123.

78. Driscoll, *How Catholic Exorcists*, 304.

79. Amorth, *An Exorcist*, 46–47.

80. Driscoll, *How Catholic Exorcists*, 114.

81. Ibid.

82. USCCB, http://www.usccb.org/prayer-and-worship/sacraments-and-sacramentals/sacramentals-blessings/exorcism.cfm.

83. Fortea, *Interview with an Exorcist*, 79.

84. Ibid.

85. Euteneuer, 101.

86. Ibid.

87. Amorth, *An Exorcist*, 139.

88. Fortea, *Interview with an Exorcist*, 110–111.

89. Driscoll, *How Catholic Exorcists,* 149.

90. Ibid., 108.

91. Amorth, *An Exorcist*, 75–76.

92. Euteneuer, *Exorcism*, 15.

93. Amorth, *An Exorcist*, 72.

94. Ibid., 84.

95. Euteneuer, *Exorcism*, 194.

96. Amorth, *An Exorcist*, 49, 112.

97. Fortea, *Interview with an Exorcist*, 109.

98. Euteneuer, *Exorcism*, 182.

99. Amorth, *An Exorcist*, 49, 112.

100. Ibid., 169.

101. Euteneuer, 183–184.

102. Ibid.

103. Ibid.

104. Amorth, 116.

105. Ibid., 74–75.

106. Fortea, *Interview with an Exorcist*, 79–80.

107. Euteneuer, *Exorcism*, 15.

108. Ibid., 191–192.

109. Ibid., 15.

110. Christian Post. http://www.christianpost.com/news/catholic-churchs-top-exorcist-claims-he-rid-world-of-160000-de-mons-96794/.

111. Amorth, *An Exorcist*, 134.

112. Ibid., 139.

113. USCCB, http://www.usccb.org/prayer-and-worship/sacraments-and-sacramentals/sacramentals-blessings/exorcism.cfm.

114. http://www.nsc-chariscenter.org/AboutCCR/; http://www.ccr.org.uk/duquesne.htm

115. See Michael Scanlan and Randall Cirner, *Deliverance from Evil Spirits* (Ann Arbor, MI: Servant Books, 1980). Francis MacNutt, *Deliverance from Evil Spirits* (Grand Rapids, MI: Chosen Books, 1995). Ann Ross Fitch and Paul Robert DeGrandis, S.S.J., *Walking in the Light* (M.A.R.Y. Ministries, 1993).

116. http://www.christendom-awake.org/pages/dombenedict/book-pray/pray-5.htm; http://christusimperat.org/en/node/11845.

117. Oblates and Missioners of St. Michael website. http://www.saint-mike.org/stmike/bios/brojp/.

118. Christopher Burbach, "Intercessors of the Lamb Closed," *World Herald*, October 16, 2010, http://www.omaha.com/article/20101015/NEWS01/710169943#intercessors-of-the-lamb-closed.

119. Scanlan and Cirner, *Deliverance from Evil Spirits,* 47–48.

120. Terry Ann Modica, *Overcoming the Power of the Occult* (Milford, OH: Faith Publishing, 1996), 193.

121. Ibid., 162.

122. John LaBriola, *Onward Catholic Soldier* (Luke 1:38 Publishing, 2008), 302.

123. Ibid., 303.

124. Euteneuer, *Exorcism*, 144.

125. Leon-Joseph Suenenes, *Renewal and the Powers of Darkness* (London: Darton, Longman, and Todd, 1983), 96. The foreword to this book was written by Pope Benedict XVI.

126. Modica, *Overcoming the Power*, 174.

127. Neal Lozano, *Unbound: A Practical Guide to Deliverance* (Grand Rapids, MI: Chosen Books, 2003), 85–94.

128. LaBriola, *Onward Catholic Soldier*, 292.

129. Euteneuer, *Exorcism*, 141.

130. Ibid., 142.

131. Lozano, *Unbound*, 200.

132. Ibid., 202.

133. LaBriola, *Onward Catholic Soldier*, 285.

134. Ibid., 287.

135. Euteneuer, *Exorcism*, 144–145.

136. Ibid.

137. USCCB, http://www.usccb.org/prayer-and-worship/sacraments-and-sacramentals/sacramentals-blessings/exorcism.cfm.

138. Daniel Van Slyke, "The Ancestry and Theology of the Rite of Major Exorcism (1999/2004)," *Antiphon*, 10, no. 1: 70–16.

139. LaBriola, *Onward Catholic Soldier*, 300.

140. Ibid.

141. Ibid., 30–32.

142. Scanlan and Cirner, *Deliverance from Evil Spirits*, 78.

143. Lozano, *Unbound*, 177–182.

144. Modica, *Overcoming the Power*, 174.

145. Pastorally, it would be insensitive to say this to those who are grieving. One can simply say instead that it is hoped that their loved one is in heaven, and that one should keep praying for the souls of those who have passed.

146. *Summa Theologica*, III, 79, 6.

147. Driscoll, *How Catholic Exorcists,* 282.

148. *Summa Theologica*, I, 64, 4.

149. Forgive my cynicism, but in my experience as a hospital chaplain for over ten years, I find that such "healing" priests carefully avoid hospital visits.

150. Rite of Exorcism, 1999, *Praenotanda*, section 16.

151. USCCB, http://www.usccb.org/prayer-and-worship/sacraments-and-sacramentals/sacramentals-blessings/exorcism.cfm.

152. Amorth, *An Exorcist*, 43, 169.

153. Aumann, *Spiritual Theology*, 401–402.

154. Ibid.

155. USCCB, http://www.usccb.org/prayer-and-worship/sacraments-and-sacramentals/sacramentals-blessings/exorcism.cfm.

156. Elizabeth Bowman, "Clinical and Spiritual Effects of Exorcism

in Fifteen Patients with Multiple Personality Disorder," *Dissociation* 6, no. 4 (December 1993), 222–238.